WWW.WEALTHYKIDS

From Piggy Banks to Stocks

The Ultimate Guide for a Young Investor

MAYA CORBIC, CPA, CA

Copyright © 2023 Maja "Maya" Corbic

All rights reserved. No part of this book may be reproduced in any form or by any electronic or mechanical means, including information storage and retrieval systems, without permission in writing from the author, except by a reviewer, who may quote brief passages in a review.

To order copies of From Piggy Banks to Stocks or to book Maya Corbic as the speaker for your next event, contact us at: frompiggybankstostocks@gmail.com
www.FromPiggyBanksToStocks.com

Discounts will be offered for bulk orders.

ISBN: 978-1-7389632-0-1 (Paperback)
ISBN: 978-1-7389632-1-8 (ePub)

Project management by M.K. Williams, Author Your Ambition
Cover and text design by Cyra K.
Edited by Sara Bruya

All content reflects opinion at a given time and can change as time progresses. All information should be taken as an opinion and should not be misconstrued for tax, financial, legal, or investing advice.

Everyone's situation is different, and not all investment strategies or products discussed may be appropriate for you.

First edition 2023.

To my own children and all the children of the world:

Regardless of who you are and where you come from, with a little bit of dedication, you can learn how to invest and create wealth.

There is a millionaire in you waiting to awaken.

TABLE OF CONTENTS

GLOSSARY

INTRODUCTION 1

CHAPTER 1: Why Should I Invest? 3

What is investing 4
Why do we need to invest 5
What is interest 5
What is inflation 7
How inflation affects your purchasing power 9
What is an emergency fund 12

CHAPTER 2: When Should I Invest? 16

Why now is the ideal time to begin investing 17
What is compound interest 18
What is the Rule of 72 24

CHAPTER 3: Meet the Key Players 28

What is the stock market 29
Public companies 30
Expenses and revenues 31
Profit and loss 32
Private companies 35
Why do companies go public 36

TABLE OF CONTENTS

What is a stock ticker symbol 39
Stock exchange 41
Shareholders 43
Brokerages 49
Investment Advisor 52
Robo Advisor 52
Invest on your own 54

CHAPTER 4: Learn About Capital Gains and
Capital Losses 56
What are capital gains and capital losses 57
Realized and unrealized capital gains 59
Realized and unrealized capital losses 62
Timing the market 65

CHAPTER 5: Discover Dividends 68
What are dividends 69
How often do companies pay dividends 73
What are financial statements 74
Dividend investors 75
Blue-chip companies 76
Dividend aristocrats and dividend kings 77

TABLE OF CONTENTS

CHAPTER 6: Understand Market Concepts 81
Investment vocabulary and terminology 82
The bull market and bear market 83
Market correction 85
Market crash 86
Hawkish and dovish policies 87

CHAPTER 7: Explore Different Investment Products 91
What are investment products 92
Risk tolerance 93
Goals and time horizon 95
Short-term investing 96
Long-term investing 96
Investment portfolio 96
Diversification 97
Term deposits 98
Bonds 99
Stocks 100
Mutual funds 101
Index funds and exchange-traded funds 102
Selecting investments 105

ANSWER KEY 111

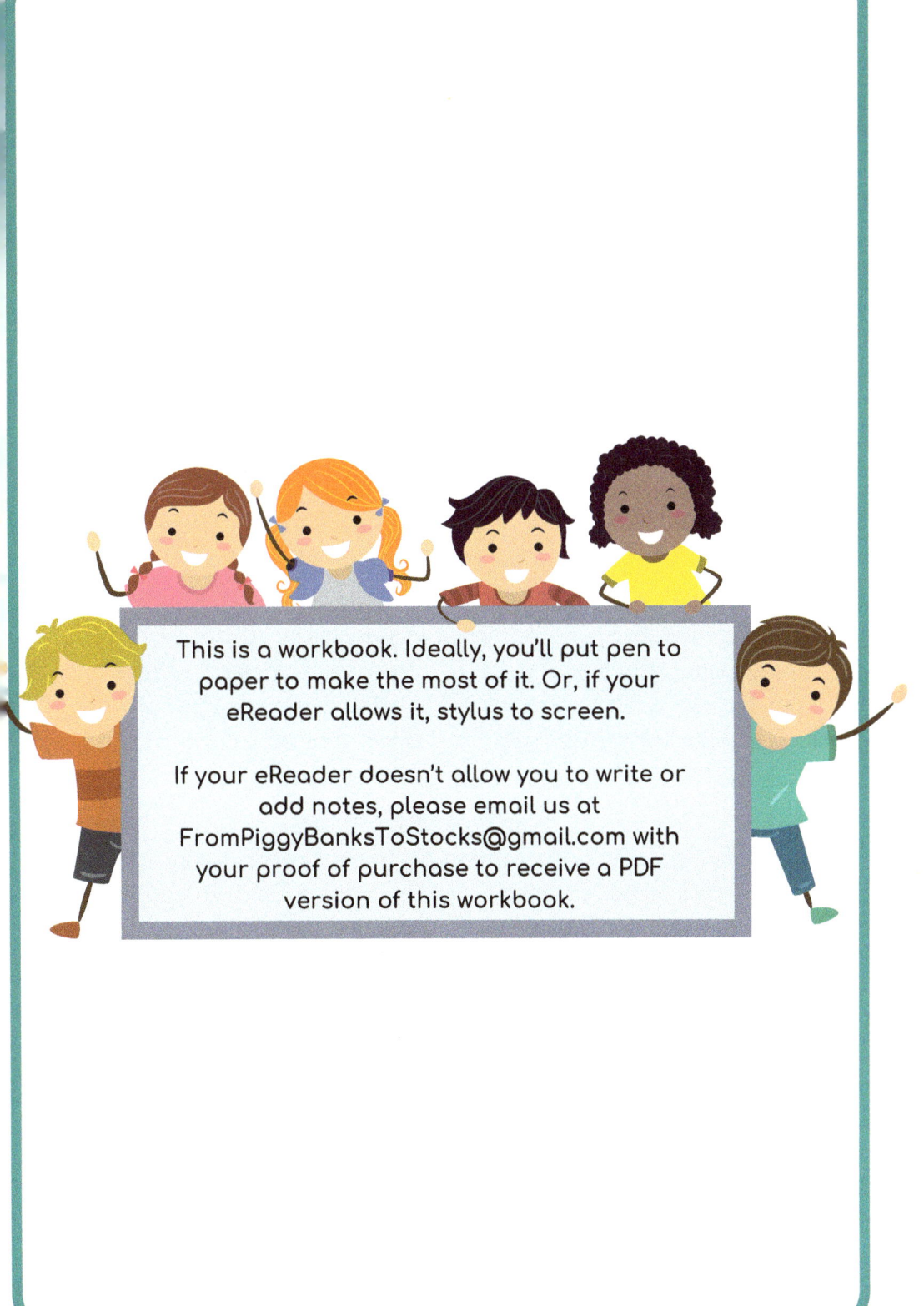

This is a workbook. Ideally, you'll put pen to paper to make the most of it. Or, if your eReader allows it, stylus to screen.

If your eReader doesn't allow you to write or add notes, please email us at FromPiggyBanksToStocks@gmail.com with your proof of purchase to receive a PDF version of this workbook.

GLOSSARY

Let's learn some new words!

As you go through this book, you may see some words that you don't know. No worries! You can use this glossary to help you understand what they mean.

B

Bear market
is when the prices of stocks are going down and people may be feeling sad or worried about their investments

Blue-chip companies
are big and strong companies that have been around for a long time and are known for being very successful

Bond
is like a loan where you give money to the government or a company and they promise to pay you back with extra money (interest) after a certain amount of time

Boom (market boom)
is when the prices of things like stocks, houses, and goods are going up and people are feeling happy and optimistic

Broker
a person who helps people buy and sell investment products by connecting buyers and sellers, like a middleman

Brokerage
an organization that charges fees for buying and selling investment products on behalf of shareholders

Bull market
is when the prices of stocks are going up and people may be feeling happy or excited about their investments

Business founder
a person who starts their own company. They come up with an idea for a product or a service and then work hard to make it successful

C

Capital
the money that a company or a person has to invest or use to make more money

Capital gains
extra money that happens when you can sell something for more money than what you originally paid for it

Capital losses
the opposite of capital gains. It is a loss of money because you can sell something for less than what you originally paid for it

Certificate of deposit (CD)
a special kind of bank account where you put your money in for a period of time, and the bank pays you extra money (interest) for leaving it there

D

Diversification
not putting all your money in one place, but spreading it out among different investments

Dividend
money that a company pays to people who own its stock, usually as a portion of the company's profits

Dividend aristocrats
companies that have paid out dividends consistently for at least 25 years

Dividend kings
companies that have paid out dividends consistently for at least 50 years

Dovish
interest rates are lowered by policymakers in order to stimulate growth in the economy

Due diligence
doing your research before making an important decision

E

Economy
is like a big system that includes all the ways that people and businesses buy and sell things, make money, and help each other out

ETF
a collection of different stocks or bonds that you can buy together instead of buying them separately. It's like a big basket of investment products that you can buy all at once

Expense
what you pay for with your money, like buying toys or food

F

Financial Statements
documents that show how well a company's business is doing

Fractional shares
owning a small piece of a share of company instead of the whole share

G

Guaranteed Investment Certificate (GIC)
a special kind of bank account where you put your money in for a period of time, and the bank pays you extra money (interest) for leaving it there

H

Hawkish
interest rates are raised by policymakers in order to encourage people and companies to be more careful about borrowing and spending money

I

Index (Stock Market Index)
a group of important stocks that people watch to see how well the stock market is doing overall

Index Fund
a special kind of investment that lets you own a little bit of all the important stocks in a stock market index, so you can make money when the index goes up

Inflation
when the prices of things like toys, candy, and even houses go up over time, so you might have to spend more money to buy the same thing later

Interest
a fee that you get paid for letting someone else use your money, or that you have to pay for borrowing someone else's money

Investing
using your money to make more money

Investment advisor
a person who provides investment advice to people

Investment product
something you can buy with your money that may help you make more money

Investors
people who use their money to buy things like stocks, businesses, etc. with the goal of making more money

M

Market (Stock Market)
a place where people buy and sell things. The stock market is like a store where people buy and sell tiny pieces of ownership in big companies

Market correction
when the prices of tiny pieces of ownership in companies (share prices) go down a little bit, which can be a normal and healthy part of the stock market

Market crash
lots of people are selling their tiny pieces (shares) of ownership in companies all at once, which can make the prices of those pieces (share prices) go down very quickly

Mitigation
doing things to make a bad situation less bad. It's like taking steps to protect yourself from harm

Mutual fund
a type of investment where lots of people put their money together to buy tiny pieces of ownership in many different companies all at once

P

Portfolio
the group of investment products that you own

Private company
a type of company that is owned by one person or a small group of people and no one else can buy pieces of ownership in it on the stock market

Profit
the extra money a person or company makes after paying for expenses

Public company
a type of company that anyone can buy pieces of ownership in on the stock market

R

Realized capital gain
when someone sells something they own for more money than they originally paid for it

Realized capital loss
when someone sells something they own for less money than they originally paid for it

Recession
when the economy is not doing well, and many people and businesses have a hard time making money

Recession-proof
when a company or a person is able to keep making money even if other people and businesses are having a hard time during a recession

Revenue
money a company makes by selling things or providing services to people

Risk tolerance
how comfortable someone is with the idea of possibly losing money when they make an investment

Robo-advisor
a computer program that helps people make decisions about what to do with their money, like how to invest it

S

Securities
various types of investment products that people can buy and sell

Shares
pieces of ownership of a company that you can buy

Shareholders
people who own tiny pieces of a company by buying shares of stock, and can get a share of the profits if the company does well or lose their money if the company does not do well

Stock
represents ownership of a small part of a company and possibly making money if the company does well

Stock exchange
a place where stocks are traded. It's like a special marketplace

Stock market
represents all of the stocks that trade in a particular region or country

Stock ticker
a way to show the current price and other information about a company's shares on a screen, like a scoreboard at a game

T

Term deposit
Putting money in a bank account for a fixed amount of time, and usually getting more money back at the end

U

Unrealized capital gain
when someone has an opportunity to sell something they own for more money than they originally paid for it, but they have not sold it yet

Unrealized capital loss
when the value of something you own is worth less money than what you originally paid for it, but you haven't actually sold it yet

Yield
the amount of money you make from your investment each year

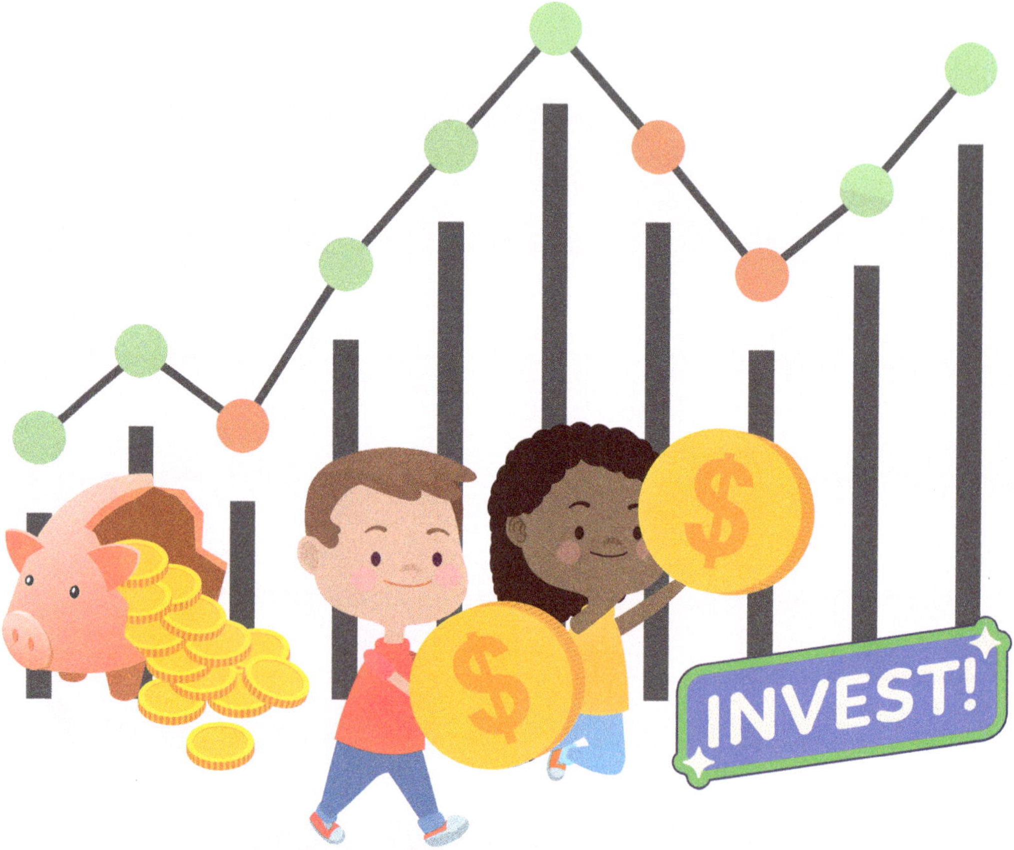
INVEST!

Introduction

How can parents ensure their children have a financially secure future? The solution came to me while I faced my own money struggles. As a first-generation immigrant who lived in shelters and government housing and worked multiple jobs, I quickly understood that investing money was the way to break the cycle of poverty.

At first, it was overwhelming. My background as a CPA gave me little in terms of foundational knowledge for investing. Hiring a financial advisor and reading several books helped me discover that the process is not as complex as I feared. I searched for ways to pass on this wealth of knowledge to my children. I wanted them to embrace investing and not be intimidated by it. I also needed to figure out how kids can learn about investing in an easy way. That's how I became inspired to write this book.

This book simplifies the basics of investing for parents and children alike. On these pages, you will find not only explanations for seemingly complicated topics and concepts but also various activities to strengthen your knowledge.

My hope is that this book will inspire you to start investing and empower you to secure a financially successful future for generations. Let's get started!

> The expert in anything was once a beginner.

— Helen Hayes

CHAPTER 1:

Why Should I Invest?

CHAPTER 1
WHY SHOULD I INVEST?

WHAT IS INVESTING?

Investing is using your money to make more money.

It is one of the best ways to start planning for your future and achieve your money goals.

This may include paying for your:

| COLLEGE | DREAM HOME | CAR |

WHY DO WE NEED TO INVEST?

Let's pretend you have $1,000.

You are debating whether you should:

a) Buy a new computer

b) Put it in a savings account

c) Invest it

What is the best thing to do with this money? Let's find out!

BUT FIRST, WE NEED TO TALK ABOUT...

WHAT IS INTEREST?

Interest is like a reward you get for letting someone borrow your money. When you put your money in a bank account, the bank uses it to make more money.
They are able to give you a little bit of extra money, called interest, as a thank you for letting them use your money.

How much interest you earn from the bank may change. It can go up or down.

1: Why Should I Invest?

SO, WHAT HAPPENS IF YOU LEAVE YOUR MONEY IN A SAVINGS ACCOUNT?

Let's go back to pretending that you have $1,000. You decide not to purchase the computer. Instead, you want to save the money in the savings account.

Let's see how much interest you'll earn by keeping $1,000.00 in the savings account for the whole year if a bank gives you 2% interest.

> Please use a calculator or ask an adult for help with this calculation if this was not covered by your math curriculum yet.

Savings x Interest Rate = Interest Earned

$1,000.00 x 2% = $_____

How much money will you have in your savings account by the end of the year?

Savings + Interest Earned = Total Amount You'll Have by the End of the Year

$1,000.00 + $_____ = $_____

What are your thoughts on the interest you've earned? Are you happy with it?

....

....

6   1: Why Should I Invest?

NOW, LET'S TALK ABOUT...

WHAT IS INFLATION?

Inflation is the rising cost of goods and services over a period of time.

What you need to know about inflation:

it makes things **more expensive** now than before

it is almost **always happening**

it **decreases your purchasing power**, which can make you buy less stuff with the same amount of money

it's like a **silent thief** (you may not even notice that it is decreasing the value of your money)

ⓘ IMPORTANT FOR YOU TO KNOW:

The inflation and savings account interest rates used in this workbook may not reflect the current rates, because they keep changing over time. The rates used here are examples for educational purposes only.

1: Why Should I Invest?

If you had a time machine and you went back in time, you could see how inflation increased the price of this chocolate bar over the years.

$0.99	$1.25	$2.15
YEAR 2000	YEAR 2010	YEAR 2022

In 2000, you could buy a chocolate bar for one dollar, whereas, in 2022, it costs more than twice as much.

Due to inflation, it is expected that this chocolate bar will cost even more in the next ten years!

WHY DO YOU NEED TO LEARN ABOUT INFLATION?

It helps you make better decisions about your money.

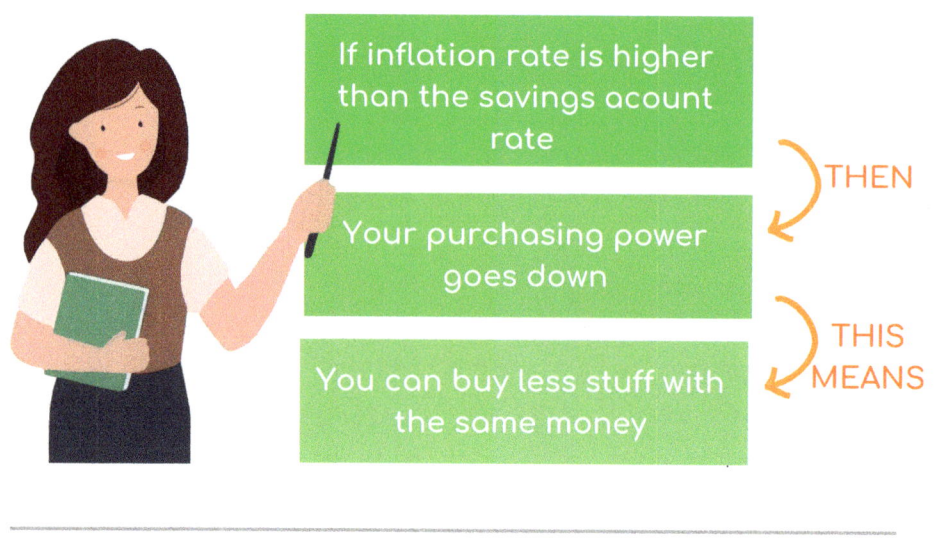

If inflation rate is higher than the savings acount rate

THEN

Your purchasing power goes down

THIS MEANS

You can buy less stuff with the same money

1: Why Should I Invest?

HOW INFLATION AFFECTS YOUR PURCHASING POWER

Let's go back to pretending that you have $1,000. You originally decided to save the money in a savings account for the year and buy the computer later.

Let's figure out what happened to the cost of the computer due to inflation over the year. For this example, we will use the inflation rate of 6.3%.

Please use the calculator or ask an adult for help with this calculation if this was not covered by your math curriculum yet.

Computer Cost x Inflation Rate = Increase in Cost Over the Year

$1,000.00 x 6.3% = $_____

What is the total cost of the computer by the end of the year?

Original Cost + Increase in Cost Over Year = Computer Cost at the End of the Year

$1,000.00 + $_____ = $_____

What are your thoughts on the increase in the cost of the computer due to inflation?

....

....

1: Why Should I Invest?

HOW INFLATION DECREASES THE VALUE OF OUR MONEY

SAVINGS ACCOUNT — Beginning of the year: $1,000.00
NEW COMPUTER — Beginning of the year: $1,000.00

Interest: 2% — End of the year: $1,020.00
Inflation: 6.3% — End of the year: $1,063.00

PURCHASING POWER LOSS = $43.00

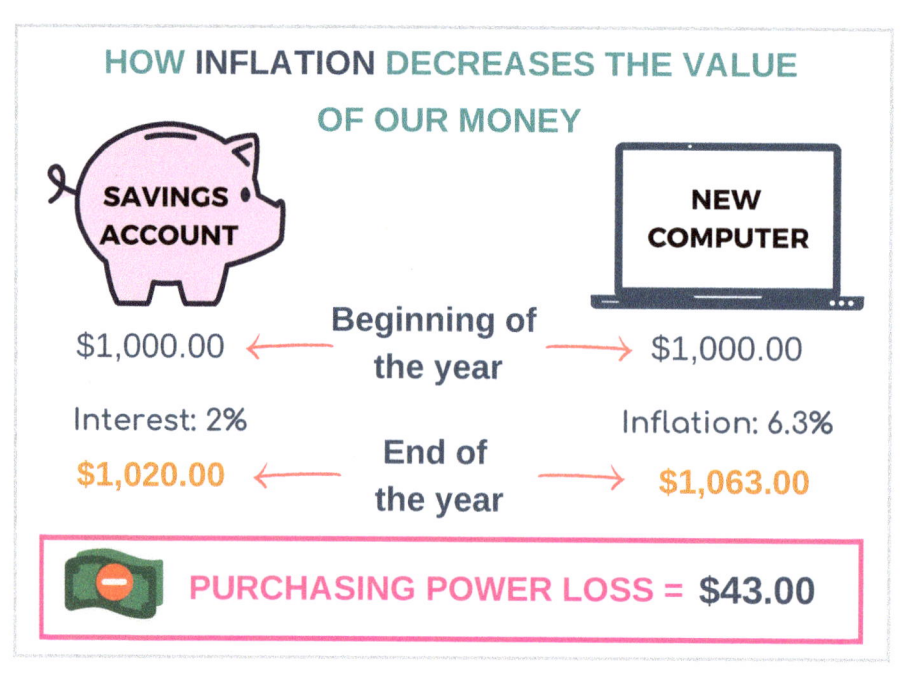

What happened when you left your $1,000 in the savings account for a year?

- At the beginning of the year, you had $1,000
- You decided to keep the money in the savings account at an interest rate of 2%.
- At the end of the year, you earned $20 in interest (see page 6)

How did your money lose purchasing power?

- At the beginning of the year, you had enough money to buy the computer, which cost $1,000
- The cost of the computer increased by $63 due to 6.3% inflation by the end of the year (see page 9)
- The money that you kept in the savings account lost purchasing power by $43 ($1,063 - $1,020) and you can no longer buy the same computer.

1: Why Should I Invest?

We need to invest outside of a savings account because our money:

- ☑ can earn more elsewhere
- ☑ can beat inflation and prevent purchasing power loss

What do you think about this?

....
. .
....

PROTECT YOUR SAVINGS FROM LOSING VALUE.

Savings accounts are not the best choice for keeping your money over a long period.

Usually, their interest rates are lower than the inflation rate, and this reduces your purchasing power.

INVESTING ELSEWHERE MAY BE A BETTER OPTION TO GROW YOUR MONEY FOR A LONGER PERIOD.

However, if you want to keep money on hand that you can use immediately or in the near future, savings accounts are still helpful.

1: Why Should I Invest?

YOU MAY WANT TO CONSIDER SETTING UP AN EMERGENCY FUND.

It's good to keep your emergency fund money in a high-yield (or high-interest) savings account so that it can earn you as much money as possible.

WHAT IS AN EMERGENCY FUND?

An emergency fund is money set aside for financial safety or unexpected expenses.

This money is intended to be used in case of an emergency, such as:

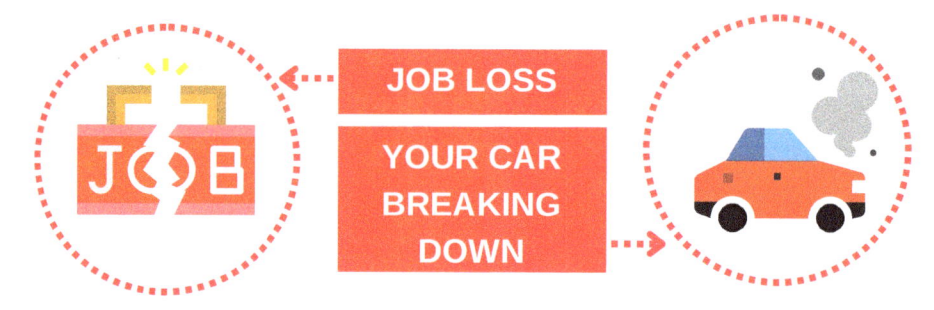

JOB LOSS

YOUR CAR BREAKING DOWN

Why do you need to know about this? Isn't this for adults?

This is important to learn because it is something you may want to have or prepare for in the future.

So, how much should be put aside for an emergency fund?

You should have enough money set aside to cover 3 to 6 months of expenditures such as groceries, electricity, water bills, car payments, etc.

What happens if you invest your emergency fund instead of keeping it in a savings account?

If you do this, you may be tempted to sell your investments to cover the unforeseen expenses.

❌ **INVESTING YOUR EMERGENCY FUND IS NOT A WISE DECISION.**

The *prices of investments go up and down,* and you may be selling them when the price is down and lose a lot of money.

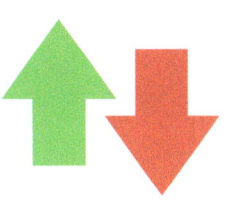

✅ **IT IS BETTER TO KEEP THE EMERGENCY FUND MONEY IN A HIGH-YIELD SAVINGS ACCOUNT.**

We do not know when an emergency will occur, so even if your money isn't earning as much due to the low-interest rate, it's best to keep it in a high-yield savings account.

Emergency funds and savings for short-term goals are the only money that we should be keeping in the savings account because we can access them quickly.

This is because the ups and downs of other investments cannot be predicted.

1: Why Should I Invest?

Let's review what you've learned so far!

PROS of a Savings Account	CONS of a Savings Account
✓	✗
✓	✗
✓	✗
✓	✗
✓	✗

Calculate how much money your investment of $1,000 will earn if you invest it at a 10% interest rate.

_ _ f _ _ t _ _ _ is the rising cost of goods and services over some time.

Do an internet search and find out how much a dozen eggs cost in 1990 and how much it costs now.

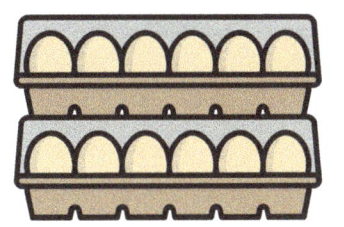

_____

_ _ t _ _ e _ _ is the money you get back for letting someone use your money.

1: Why Should I Invest?

CHAPTER 2:

When Should I Start Investing?

CHAPTER 2
WHEN SHOULD I START INVESTING?

WHY NOW IS THE IDEAL TIME TO BEGIN INVESTING!

Your money will have more time to grow if you start investing earlier.

You may be asking: What's the difference between investing now and investing later?

Let's get to know the magic of compound interest!

> Compound interest is the eighth wonder of the world. He who understands it, earns it … he who doesn't … pays it.
>
> Albert Einstein

2: When Should I Start Investing?

WHAT IS COMPOUND INTEREST?

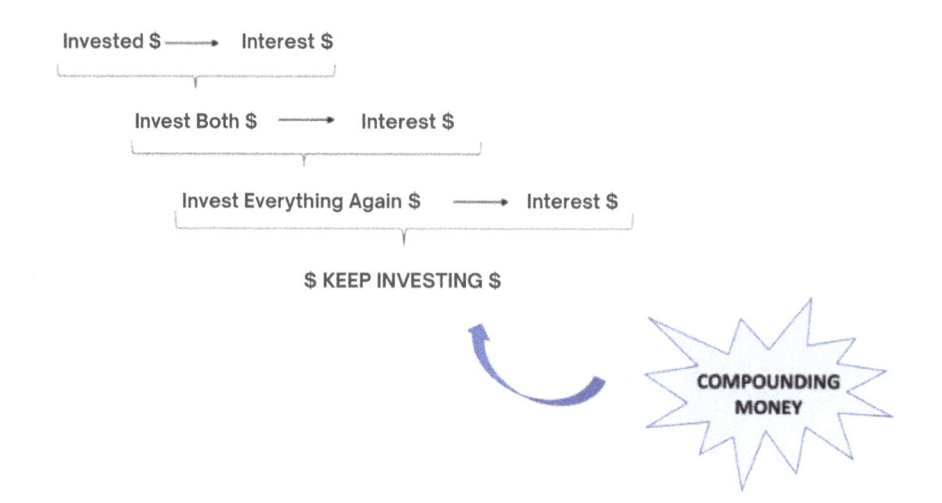

Invested $ → Interest $

Invest Both $ → Interest $

Invest Everything Again $ → Interest $

$ KEEP INVESTING $

COMPOUNDING MONEY

Compound interest is a cool concept that allows your money to make even more money. This is because you earn interest on the original amount you invested, and then you earn interest on that interest, which grows your money further.

Not only are you earning from the money you initially put in, but also from all of the money you've made along the way.

MAGIC OF COMPOUNDING

Year	Amount at Start	Interest	Amount at End
0 (Now)	$1,000.00	($1,000.00 x 10% =) **$100.00**	$1,100.00
1	$1,100.00	($1,100.00 x 10% =) **$110.00**	$1,210.00
2	$1,210.00	($1,210.00 x 10% =) **$121.00**	$1,331.00
3	$1,331.00	($1,331.00 x 10% =) **$133.00**	$1,464.10
4	$1,464.10	($1,464.10 x 10% =) **$146.41**	$1,610.51
5	$1,610.51		

Imagine you have $1,000 earning 10% interest annually (which means yearly).

At the end of the first year, you'll have $1,100.00, while at the end of the second year, you'll have $1,210.00.

You made $100 on the initial investment alone. Then you kept that $100 invested, and you earned $10.00 on it, giving you a total of $110.00 in earnings at the end of the second year.

At the end of the tenth year, the $1,000 will grow to $2,593.74!

That $1,000 went to work for you and kept earning you more money each year without you working or doing anything. The $1,000 was working for you while you were sleeping! By the end of year 10, it earned you an additional $1,593.74!

Pretty awesome, right?

2: When Should I Start Investing?

THIS IS WHY COMPOUND INTEREST IS POWERFUL

Compound interest and investing allow you to earn money without working for it.

WORKING AT A JOB	INVESTING
Exchange time for money	Our money earns us money
How much we work, determines how much we earn	Get paid regardless of how much we work
If we don't work, we don't get paid	We can be on a beach, sleeping or playing ball while our invested money is working for us

INVESTING NOW, RATHER THAN LATER.

Compound interest can be used to your advantage when you're young and have plenty of time on your side.

The longer you invest your money, the more it grows, and it can make you wealthy.

WHY INVESTING EARLIER IS IMPORTANT

This is the story of two friends who started investing at different times and, because of that, earned different amounts of money.

MEET SILVIA AND MARY

SILVIA	MARY
• Starts contributing to her investments at the age of 14 and stops at 30. • Contributes $1,000 each year for 16 years (total invested = $16,000) • The money is left to grow in the investment account until she is 65 years old. By that time, her money has grown to approximately $1,010,283.	• Starts contributing to her investments at the age of 35 and stops at 65. • Contributes $5,000 each year for 30 years (total invested = $150,000). • The money is worth approximately $822,470 when she turns 65.

2: When Should I Start Investing?

	Silvia	Mary
Starts investing (age)	14	35
Stops contributing (age)	30	65
Total years contributing	16	30
Contributed each year	$1,000	$5,000
Total contributed	$16,000	$150,000
Interest rate	10%	10%
Investment value (age 65)	**$1,010,283**	**$822,470**

Summary:

Silvia has more money by age 65 than Mary even though she only contributed money to her investments for 16 years, while Mary did it for 30 years. Also, Silvia only contributed $16,000 while Mary contributed $150,000.

At age 65 Silvia has more money than Mary for 2 reasons:

1. Started investing earlier
2. Took advantage of the compound interest

IT'S IMPORTANT TO START INVESTING EARLY.

You don't even have to wait until you've saved up $1,000.00 to start investing.

You can begin by putting aside one or two dollars per day and invest them at the end of the month.

COMPOUND INTEREST IS MIRACULOUS

Would you take $3 million in cash NOW, OR take one penny that doubles in value every day for 30 days?

30th day!!!

Day	Value
1	$ 0.01
2	$ 0.02
3	$ 0.04
4	$ 0.08
5	$ 0.16
6	$ 0.32
7	$ 0.64
8	$ 1.28
9	$ 2.56
10	$ 5.12
11	$ 10.24
12	$ 20.48
13	$ 40.96
14	$ 81.92
15	$ 163.84
16	$ 327.68
17	$ 655.36
18	$ 1,310.72
19	$ 2,621.44
20	$ 5,242.88
21	$ 10,485.76
22	$ 20,971.52
23	$ 41,943.04
24	$ 83,886.08
25	$ 167,772.16
26	$ 335,544.32
27	$ 671,088.64
28	$ 1,342,177.28
29	$ 2,684,354.56
30	$ 5,368,709.12

What was your original answer? Are you surprised by how much a penny is worth at the end of 30 days when it doubles in value daily?

....

....

This was a fun exercise. Unfortunately, doubling money daily is impossible. But you can increase your money by investing, which is what this book will teach you.

2: When Should I Start Investing?

WHAT IS THE RULE OF 72?

The Rule of 72 is a quick way to calculate how long it will take to double your money if it is invested at a particular interest rate.

How does it work?

To find out how many years it will take for your invested money to double, divide 72 by the interest rate that you expect to earn.

$$72 / \text{Interest Rate} = \text{Years}$$

Example

How long will it take to double your money if your investment has an interest rate of 6%?

$$72 / 6 = 12 \text{ years}$$

It will take 12 years to double your money.

DOUBLING MONEY IN THE SAVINGS ACCOUNT

How long will it take for you to double your money if you keep $1,000.00 in a savings account at a 3% interest rate per year?

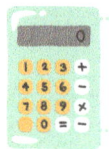

If you need help with this calculation, use the calculator or ask an adult.

$$72 / \text{Interest Rate} = \text{Years}$$

$$72 / 3 = \underline{\hspace{2cm}} \text{ years}$$

What do you think about that? Is that a long time?

....

....

24   2: When Should I Start Investing?

WOULD YOU LIKE TO DOUBLE YOUR MONEY SOONER?

If so, you may have to consider investing it outside of the savings account.

You can also use the Rule of 72 and calculate the interest rate that you need to earn in order for your investment to double over a certain period.

For example, let's say that you want to double your money in 8 years. How much should your annual (yearly) interest rate on an investment be?

To calculate that, you need to divide 72 by the number of years you want your money to double.

If you need help with this calculation, use the calculator or ask an adult.

72 / Number of Years You Want Your Money to Double = Interest Rate

72 / _____ years = _____ %

THE ADVANTAGE OF USING THE RULE OF 72.

You can use the Rule of 72 to create an investment strategy that will help you achieve your financial goals.

2: When Should I Start Investing?

Let's review what you've learned so far!

PROS of Investing Early	CONS of Investing Early
✓	✗
✓	✗
✓	✗
✓	✗
✓	✗
✓	✗

2: When Should I Start Investing?

What is the name of the concept that allows your money to earn money on already earned money?

(Please circle the correct answer)

a. Playing games

b. Compound interest

c. Magic tricks

The Rule of _ _

is a quick way to calculate how long it will take to double our money if it is invested at a particular interest rate.

CHAPTER 3:

Meet the
Key Players

CHAPTER 3
MEET THE KEY PLAYERS

WHAT IS THE STOCK MARKET?

A stock market is a place where people around the world can come together to buy and sell things, just like any other market. In this case, they are buying and selling various types of investment products, which are also called securities.

The stock market is composed of:

Public Companies

Stock Exchanges

Shareholders

Brokerages

Investment Advisors

In this section of the workbook, you are going to learn about different participants in the stock market. It is important to understand who the participants are and how they interact with each other to successfully invest.

PUBLIC COMPANIES

To help us understand what public companies are, a boy named Mike will help us out.

Hi! I'M MIKE.

EXPENSES AND REVENUES

Mike decided to set up a lemonade stand to earn money. Before opening up for business, Mike went grocery shopping and spent $500.00 on lemons, sugar, pitchers, and other items needed to sell lemonade.

EXPENSES: $500.00

The costs of these items (needed for Mike's business to function) are called *expenses*.

REVENUE: $2,000.00

EXPENSES: $500.00

PROFIT: $1,500.00

Mike ran his lemonade stand for two months in the summer and sold a lot of lemonade. He earned $2,000.00 in sales. This is called *revenue*.

3: Meet the Key Players

PROFIT AND LOSS

Sometimes revenue (or sales) are confused with profit. Profit is different. Profit is the money that is left from Mike's sales after he deducts his expenses.

Remember Mike's $500.00 purchase of lemons, sugar, and pitchers?

For Mike to calculate his profit, Mike has to deduct $500 of expenses from his revenues of $2,000.

$$\$2,000.00 - \$500.00 = \$1,500.00$$

His profit is $1,500.

However, a business may not always make a profit. It can lose money when expenses are greater than revenues.

That is referred to as a loss.

REVENUE: $400.00

EXPENSES: $500.00

LOSS: -$100.00

An example of a loss would be if Mike spent $500 on supplies for his lemonade stand, but only sold $400 worth of lemonade. Since his expenses exceeded his lemonade sales, Mike suffered a $100 loss.

$$\$400.00 - \$500.00 = -\$100.00$$

Here is the formula to calculate profit or loss for a business:

REVENUE - EXPENSES = PROFIT OR LOSS

If the result is *positive* (revenues are greater than expenses), the business has a profit.

If the result is *negative* (revenues are lower than expenses), the business has a loss.

3: Meet the Key Players

let's practice making some calculations!

Hi! I'm Ava

Calculate the profit or loss of Ava's cupcake business. In December, just before the holidays, Ava purchased supplies to make cupcakes and spent $200. With those supplies, she baked the most delicious cupcakes, which she sold for $700.

Did Ava have a profit or loss for the month of December? If so, how much?

$700.00 - $200.00 = _____

If Ava repeated the same process from January to April, and each month she earned $700 in revenue but spent $1,000 in total on cupcake supplies, how much did she earn from December to April?

($700.00 x 5 months) - $1,000.00 = _____

PRIVATE COMPANIES

Companies can be private or public. Currently, Mike's lemonade business is a private company, because he is its only business owner.

Let's say that Mike's lemonade business is doing very well and he wants to expand it to other locations and earn more money. To do so, he needs to buy supplies to build additional lemonade stands, and he needs more pitchers, lemons, sugar, etc. Mike will also have to employ others to work the new lemonade stands for him.

| FIRST LEMONADE STAND | ADDITIONAL LEMONADE STANDS |

To expand his business, Mike needs money (which is called capital).

To obtain more capital for expansion, Mike has decided to take the company public.

3: Meet the Key Players 35

WHAT DOES IT MEAN TO GO PUBLIC?

The simplest way to explain this is that when companies go public, they are allowing anyone to buy their shares. Therefore, anyone can own a piece of that company.

And yes, even you!

WHY DO COMPANIES GO PUBLIC?

Private companies go public because they need the extra money for growth and expansion, such as paying for employees and supplies and going public allows them to raise these funds from people who want to become shareholders or owners of their company.

In this case, Mike needs more money for his lemonade company's further expansion, and he thinks that he can get that additional capital by taking his company public.

Do you know of any private companies? Think of your family members or parents' friends. Do they have businesses that are private companies?

....

....

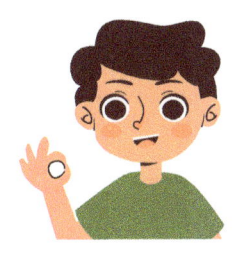

Let's see how you can apply what you've learned in the real world.

Here's a list of known public companies:

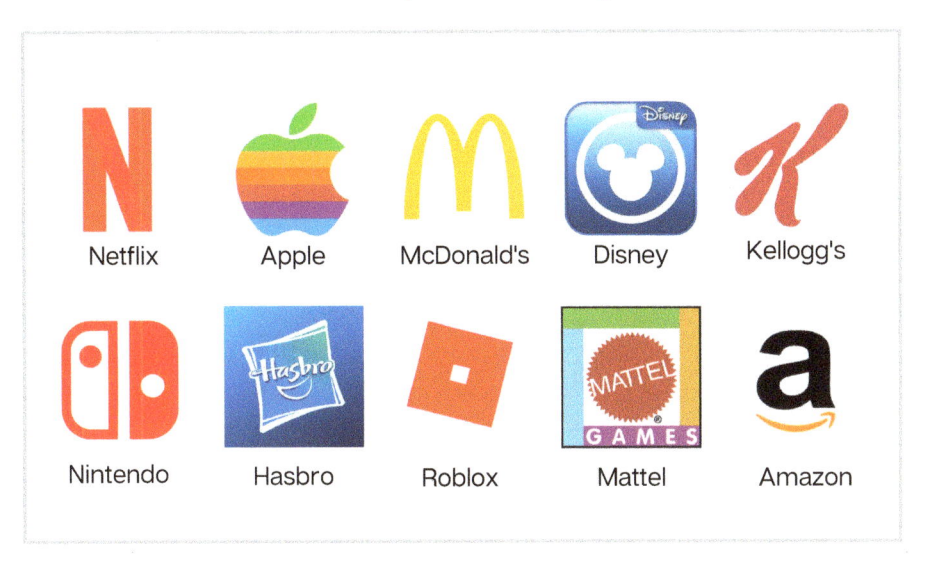

Netflix	Apple	McDonald's	Disney	Kellogg's
Nintendo	Hasbro	Roblox	Mattel	Amazon

These are just examples of public companies. This is not a recommendation for you to invest in any of these companies, but rather do your own research and due diligence before investing. Remember, never invest in something that you do not understand or have not done research on.

Do you know of any public companies other than the ones mentioned on the previous page?

Take a walk through your home, pick up various objects, and find out what companies make them. The name of the company that makes them should be listed on the label of the product. To find out which companies are public, you can use the internet. In the online search bar type the question:

Is [name of the company] a public company?

> Write down some of the public companies whose products you use in your home:

3: Meet the Key Players

WHAT IS A STOCK TICKER SYMBOL?

Stock ticker symbols are used to identify a stock from a public company. Private companies that are not listed publicly on a stock exchange do not have stock ticker symbols.

Each public company will have a unique ticker symbol. Additionally, if a company's stock is listed on several stock exchanges, each exchange may assign it a different ticker symbol.

Here are some fun stock ticker symbols for public companies:

BOOM
Dynamic Materials Corp.
Maker of explosives

DNUT
Krispy Kreme Doughnut chain

ZZ
Sealy Corp.
Mattress manufacturer

HOG
Harley-Davidson Motorcycle manufacturer

WOOF
Antech
Vet diagnostic provider

YODA
The Procure Space Satellite operators & hardware makers

3: Meet the Key Players

FINDING TICKER SYMBOLS ONLINE

If you're interested to know the stock ticker symbol of a company, use the following phrase to do an online search:

[Company Name] Stock Ticker Symbol

Let's take Roblox as an example and look up its stock ticker symbol online.

> Roblox Stock Ticker Symbol

Once you hit enter, you should be able to find Roblox's stock ticker symbol near the top of the search results:

Roblox Corp
NYSE: **RBLX** ← STOCK TICKER SYMBOL

Overview | Compare | Financials

Do the online search and find the stock ticker symbols for the companies that you are interested in. List them down below.

NAME OF COMPANY	STOCK TICKER SYMBOL
	→
	→
	→

40   3: Meet the Key Players

STOCK EXCHANGE

To go public, companies must be listed on a stock exchange.

Stock exchanges are places where stocks are traded. It's like a special marketplace.

These exchanges allow for stocks to be purchased or sold by others. This can be done in a physical space, but most stock trading nowadays is done virtually.

STOCK EXCHANGES ARE ALSO REGULATED SPACES. WHAT DOES THIS MEAN?

This means there are a lot of rules that need to be followed by companies and investors to make sure there is no fraud, scam, or anything illegal happening.

THERE ARE MANY STOCK EXCHANGES AROUND THE WORLD.

The two most popular and big stock exchanges in the United States are the National Association of Securities Dealers Automated Quotations (NASDAQ) and the New York Stock Exchange (NYSE).

In Canada, the largest stock exchange is The Toronto Stock Exchange (TSX).

Other countries have their stock exchanges as well. If you're interested in what other stock exchanges there are, you can search the following phrase online: "List of all stock exchanges in the world".

List of all stock exchanges in the world

3: Meet the Key Players

SHAREHOLDERS

Shareholders are owners of the company. If there is more than one owner of the company, they are all part-owners as they own different parts/percentages of the company.

Now let's go back and see how Mike's private lemonade company becomes a public company.

ESTIMATE OF THE LEMONADE BUSINESS VALUE: $10,000.00

BUSINESS CONSULTANT

Mike hired a special business consultant who evaluated Mike's business and stated that it is worth $10,000. In real life, calculating how much a business is worth depends on detailed and complex calculations, which will not be covered in this workbook.

3: Meet the Key Players

The $10,000 is the estimate of the lemonade business value. This estimate does not mean that Mike has $10,000 in cash from the business. That $10,000 represents the value of his business based on its previous revenues, expenses, and potential for more profit and growth.

There are a few investors who are interested in investing in the lemonade business. One of them is Ava.

Do you remember Ava from one of the previous activities?

She had profits of $2,500 from her cupcake business.

Ava saved all of her profits and wants to invest that money into Mike's lemonade business. In exchange, she expects to profit from the growth of Mike's future lemonade business.

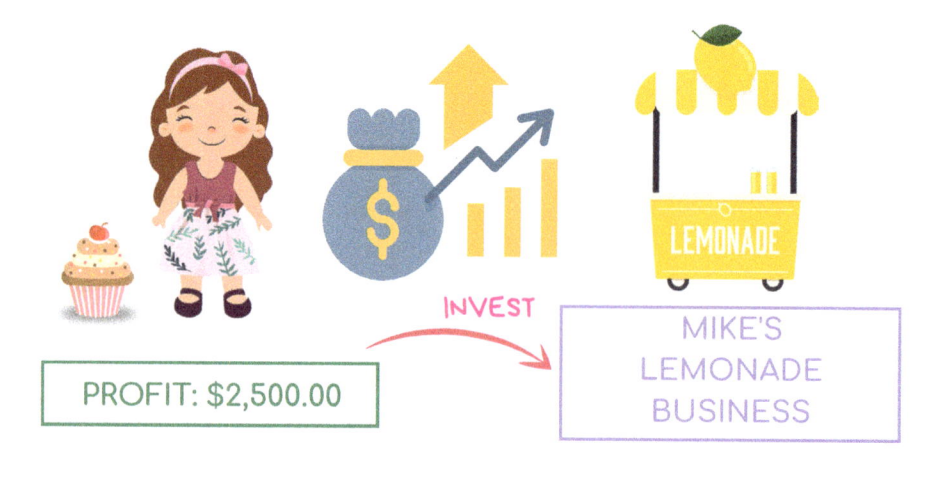

PROFIT: $2,500.00

INVEST

MIKE'S LEMONADE BUSINESS

Since Mike's lemonade company is worth $10,000, let's pretend that Mike decided to split the company into 10,000 pieces or stock shares. A share of stock is a small piece of the company that is sold to raise money. In this case, each share of stock is worth $1.

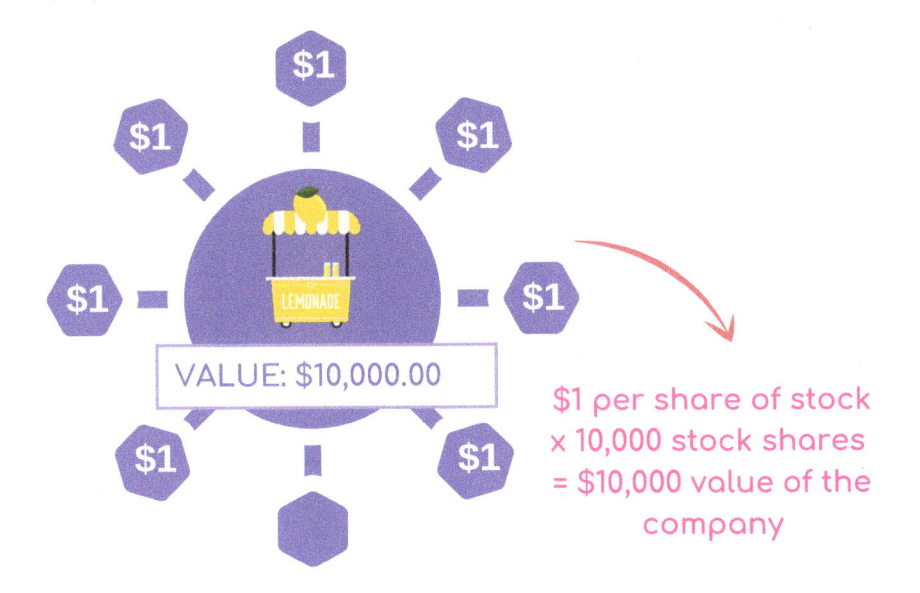

VALUE: $10,000.00

$1 per share of stock
× 10,000 stock shares
= $10,000 value of the company

How many shares can Ava buy? Let's calculate that.

$2,500 (Ava's investment) / $1 per share of stock

= 2,500 shares.

If the lemonade company only has 10,000 shares, let's calculate how much percentage-wise Ava owns.

2,500 shares / 10,000 shares = 25 × 100%

= 25% (Ava's ownership)

3: Meet the Key Players

Therefore Mike still owns 75% of the company (100% - 25% of Ava's ownership) or 7,500 shares of stock (10,000 - 2,500).

Now Ava and Mike are shareholders of the lemonade company.

As mentioned earlier, there are other investors interested in investing in the lemonade business since it has gone public. These other investors invest $2,000 in exchange for 2,000 shares or 20% of the company.

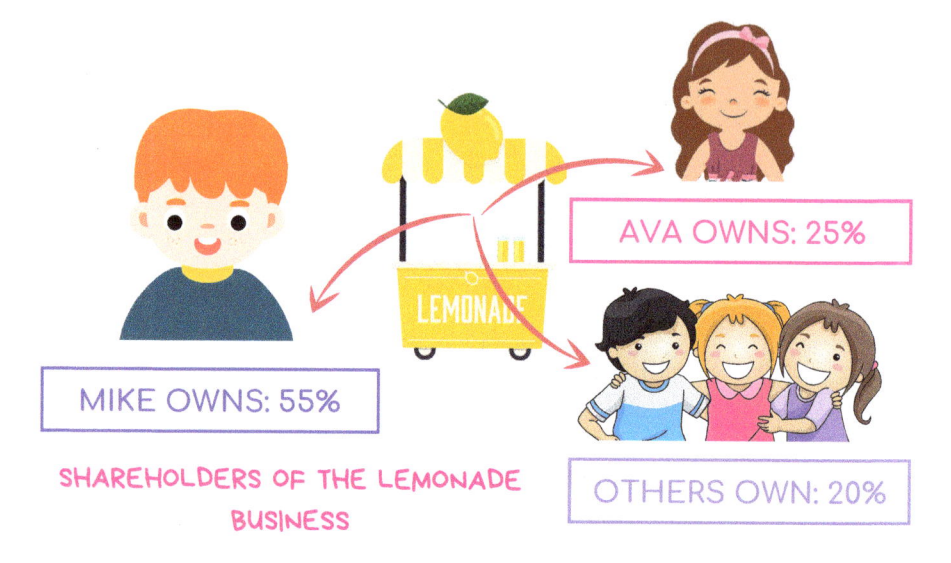

AVA OWNS: 25%

MIKE OWNS: 55%

OTHERS OWN: 20%

SHAREHOLDERS OF THE LEMONADE BUSINESS

This is the breakdown of the lemonade public company ownership:

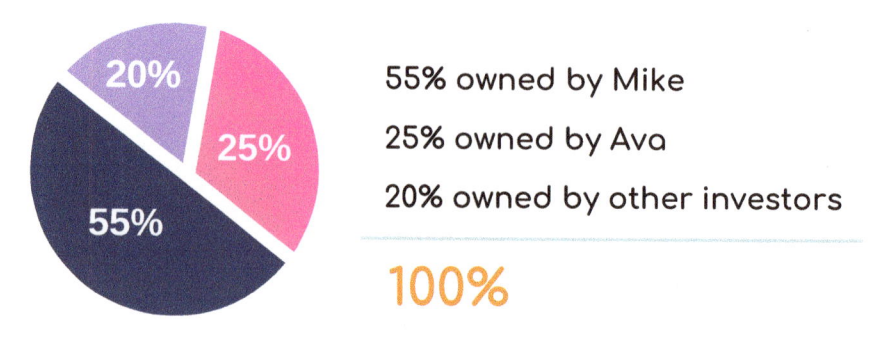

55% owned by Mike

25% owned by Ava

20% owned by other investors

100%

3: Meet the Key Players

Some shareholders can be involved in the day-to-day operations of the company and some shareholders may not be.

In this case, Mike is involved in the daily operations of the lemonade company while Ava and the other investors are not.

BUSINESS FOUNDERS WANT TO KEEP AT LEAST 51% OWNERSHIP OF THE COMPANY.

Business founders like Mike have to be careful about how much of their business they sell off to others. Usually, they want to keep at least 51% ownership of the company stock, which allows them to make decisions on behalf of the company as they have majority ownership. The majority ownership is anything over 50%.

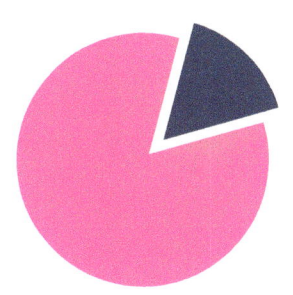

BUT WHAT HAPPENS IF BUSINESS FOUNDERS SELL 51% OR MORE OF THE COMPANY'S STOCK?

If Mike sold 51% or more of his business and only kept a small part (49% or less), he would not have as much say in important business decisions. The other shareholders who own more of the business than he does (the remaining 51%) would be able to make important decisions together, without needing Mike's approval.

3: Meet the Key Players 47

RISKS

WHEN WE INVEST OUR MONEY, WE NEED TO BE AWARE THAT WE ARE ALWAYS EXPOSED TO SOME DEGREE OF RISK.

We may lose all or part of our money if what we invested in does not work out.

It is important to note that Ava and the other investors are facing a risk that they can lose some or all of their invested money if the lemonade business does poorly in the future and shuts down.

That is why it is important to never invest our money into something that we do not understand and believe in.

BROKERAGES

Shareholders buy and sell their shares on stock exchanges through a brokerage. Some investors may use an investment advisor.

WHAT ARE BROKERAGES?

A brokerage is an organization that charges fees and commissions for buying and selling investment products on behalf of shareholders. They act as a bridge between the shareholders and the stock exchange.

SO, WHAT ARE SOME OF THE MOST WELL-KNOWN BROKERAGES?

There are many well-known brokerages in the US:

Vanguard, Fidelity, Charles Schwab, TD Ameritrade, E*Trade, etc.

Some Canadian brokerages are:

Wealthsimple, TD Waterhouse, Qtrade Investor, CIBC Investor's Edge, etc.

3: Meet the Key Players

> **ⓘ IMPORTANT FOR YOU TO KNOW:**
>
> Please note that the brokerages mentioned in this workbook are just examples and their inclusion does not imply endorsement. Always make sure that you do your research and due diligence before investing your money with a brokerage.
>
> Depending on which country you live in, you may want to do some research to find the most reputable brokerages in your country.

SOME BROKERAGES ALLOW FRACTIONAL SHARE OWNERSHIP.

What is fractional share ownership?

Some reputable public companies have a very high share price. For example, at one point in time, Amazon's share price was as high as $2,000 per share, which is quite high compared to other companies.

However, if you did not have that amount of money, you could have purchased a fraction of a share through brokerages that allow for fractional share ownership.

You could have even continued to buy fractions of the share until you purchased the full share.

HOW TO OPEN A BROKERAGE ACCOUNT

You have to be 18 years old to open a brokerage account.

If you are younger, your parent or guardian can open an account in their name for you as a beneficiary.

This can be done on most brokerage websites.

INVESTMENT ADVISOR

An investment advisor is a person who provides investment recommendations based on:

- ✅ Investment Goals
- ✅ Risk Tolerance
- ✅ Other Factors

In exchange for a fee, they can help choose the investments that are best for you.

ROBO-ADVISOR

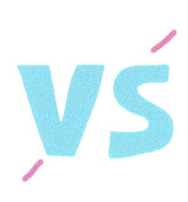

INVESTMENT ADVISOR   VS   ROBO-ADVISOR

You can choose a real live person as an investment advisor or a Robo-Advisor. Robo-Advisor is an artificial intelligence that collects information about you via an online survey and then asks you a series of questions to help you choose investments that will benefit you and help you achieve your goals.

CHOOSING THE RIGHT BROKERAGE AND INVESTMENT ADVISOR

It's important to understand how to choose the right brokerage and investment advisor so you can start thinking about how and with whom you'd like to open an account when you start buying stocks for yourself in the future.

There are many brokerages and investment advisors out there. You must do your homework before deciding where you'll be investing your money.

Here are a couple of things to think about when selecting the right broker:

1. How much are their fees?

You should consider the fees when choosing a brokerage account or an investment advisor. Even if the fees seem small, say only 2%, that is still quite high and can add up to hundreds of thousands of dollars over time.

2. How reputable, knowledgeable, and reliable are they?

Make sure to do your research and find out how long they've been in business. Can you trust them? Do they know what they're talking about?

INVEST ON YOUR OWN

YOU CAN ALSO CHOOSE TO MANAGE YOUR OWN INVESTMENTS.

Instead of using an investment advisor or robo-advisor, you can choose to manage your own investments.

To do so, you have to educate yourself about investing. As mentioned before, never invest in something that you do not understand.

Would you choose an investment advisor, robo-advisor, or manage your investments by yourself? Why?

....
....
....
....

Let's see how you can apply what you've learned in the real world.

Research various brokerage websites and select the one that is most suitable for you. Find out if they charge transaction fees (for purchasing or selling investment products), inactivity fees (when not using your account), etc.

BROKERAGE NAME	FEES	NOTES

CHAPTER 4:

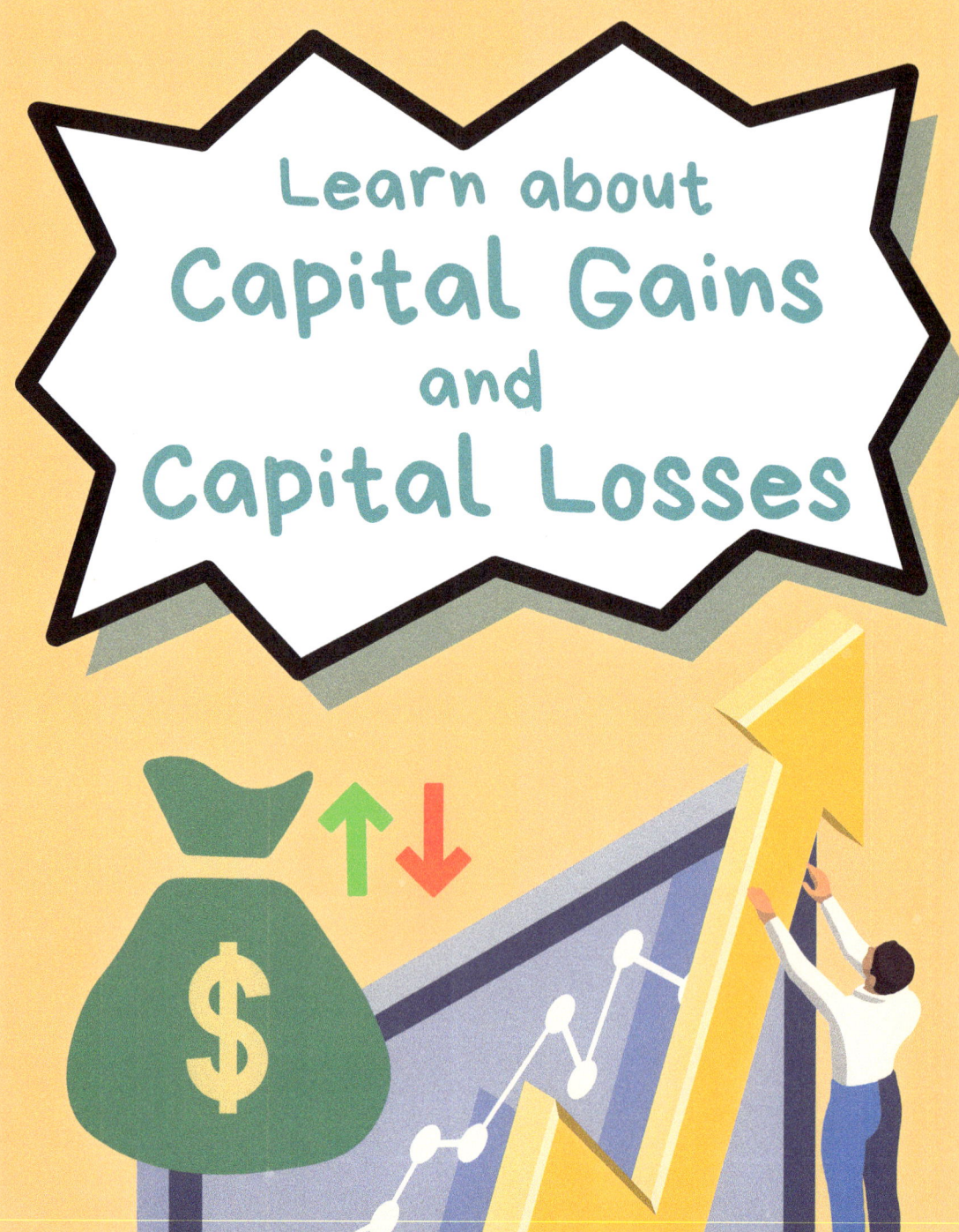

Learn about Capital Gains and Capital Losses

LET'S LEARN ABOUT CAPITAL GAINS & CAPITAL LOSSES

WHAT ARE CAPITAL GAINS AND CAPITAL LOSSES?

It is five years in the future and the lemonade public company has done well. The capital that Mike raised after the company went public was strategically invested in the expansion and the company made profits year after year.

How does this affect shareholders like Ava?

Let's find out!

The lemonade company is well-regarded in the market by other investors. They think highly of it. Other investors in the market believe that the company is now worth $50,000.

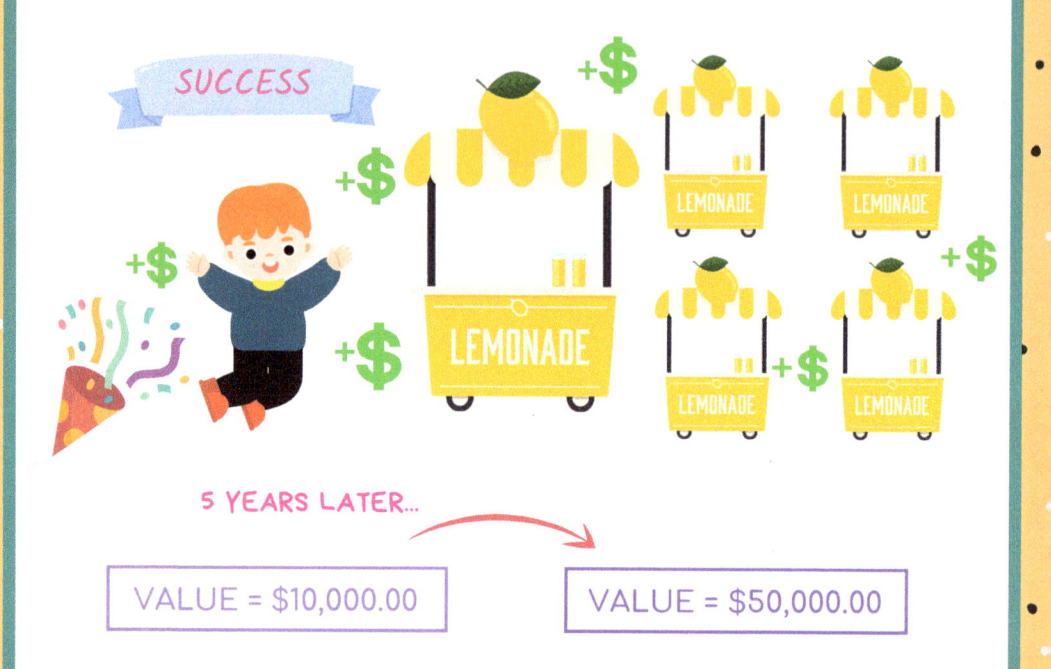

VALUE = $10,000.00

5 YEARS LATER...

VALUE = $50,000.00

That is great news. Remember five years ago that same business was worth $10,000. Therefore, it grew in value. If the business is worth $50,000 and has 10,000 shares, how much is each share worth?

Now after 5 years, each share is worth $5 ($50,000 / 10,000 shares).

4: Learn about Capital Gains and Capital Losses

REALIZED AND UNREALIZED CAPITAL GAINS

Shareholders like Ava will hold on to their shares, but at some point, they will want to sell them and earn money.

When Ava became a shareholder, she paid $1 per share. Now she can sell each of her shares for $5. What is Ava's profit per share?

Bought shares at $1.00 each share

Sells shares at $5.00 each share

CAPITAL GAIN : $4.00

Ava's profit is $4 per share ($5 - $1).

This profit is called capital gain. If Ava sells shares of the lemonade company, that gain will be called a realized capital gain, because it happened. It was realized.

If Ava decides not to sell her shares but is just calculating for fun how much her capital gain would be, then $4 per share is unrealized capital gain. It is called unrealized because it has not happened yet.

The unrealized capital gain may go up or down in the future depending on how well the lemonade company does. It will only become realized when Ava sells her shares.

4: Learn about Capital Gains and Capital Losses

Let's practice making some calculations!

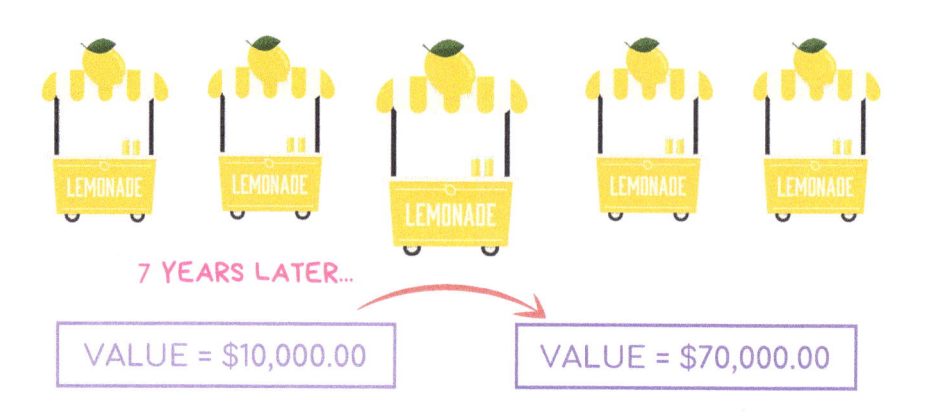

7 YEARS LATER...

VALUE = $10,000.00

VALUE = $70,000.00

Let's pretend that it is 7 years after the lemonade business went public. The business is still profitable and highly regarded by the market and other investors. They think that it is worth $70,000.

If there are still only 10,000 shares of the lemonade business, how much is each share of stock worth now?

$70,000.00 / 10,000 shares =

Help Ava calculate her capital gain if she sold her 2,500 shares at the new price of shares. Remember, she originally bought each share at $1/share.

(2,500 shares x new price per share) - Ava's initial investment =

If Ava is doing this calculation for fun but does not sell her shares, is her capital gain realized or unrealized?

4: Learn about Capital Gains and Capital Losses

REALIZED AND UNREALIZED CAPITAL LOSSES

If however, the lemonade company was not well regarded by the market and other investors, and they thought that it was only worth $6,000, how much would each share be worth?

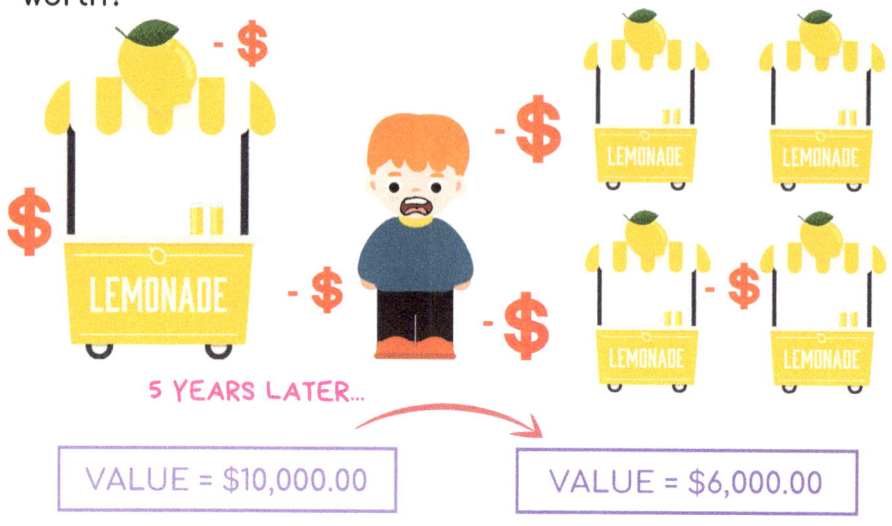

5 YEARS LATER...

VALUE = $10,000.00

VALUE = $6,000.00

$6,000 / 10,000 shares = $0.60 per share

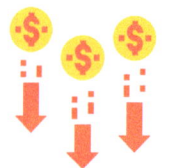

Since Ava originally paid $1 per share, and now she can only sell each share of stock for $0.60, she has a capital loss. However, this loss may be an unrealized capital loss if she does not sell her shares but holds on to them if she believes that the lemonade company will recover in value.

Alternatively, if she sells her shares, she will have a realized capital loss of $0.40 per share ($0.60 current price per share less $1 original price per share).

It is important to note that Ava does not need to sell all of her 2,500 shares at the same time. She can sell some of them now and others later.

Let's practice making some calculations!

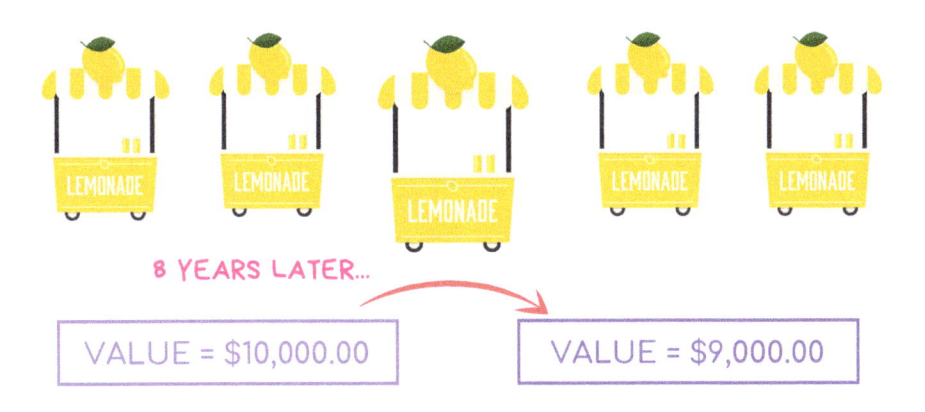

8 YEARS LATER...

VALUE = $10,000.00

VALUE = $9,000.00

Let's pretend that it is 8 years after the lemonade business went public. The business is not doing well anymore. It has suffered significant losses. The market and other investors think that it is worth $9,000.

If there are still only 10,000 shares of the lemonade business, how much is each share of stock worth now?

$9,000.00 / 10,000 shares =

4: Learn about Capital Gains and Capital Losses

Ava thinks that the lemonade business will continue to do poorly in the future. She wants to cut her losses and decides to sell her shares before they are worth even less. Calculate Ava's capital loss when she sells all 2,500 shares at the new market price of shares. Remember, she originally bought each share at $1/share.

(2,500 shares x new price per share) - Ava's initial investment =

Is this loss realized or unrealized?

TIMING THE MARKET

THE PHRASE "BUY LOW, SELL HIGH" HAS BECOME A CATCHPHRASE IN THE WORLD OF INVESTING, AND SOMETHING ALL INVESTORS STRIVE TO ACHIEVE.

But what does it mean?

Here's a quick explanation.

Everyone's goal when investing is to make money.

And if you want to make money you want to purchase investments at a low price and sell when the price is higher.

Doesn't that sound simple?

It may seem simple, but the truth is it is difficult to know when the share price is low and when it's high.

IT'S INCREDIBLY HARD TO TIME THE MARKET.

Even the most skilled investors in the world cannot time the market consistently.

You'll have to do your due diligence and research on an investment, then make your best-educated guess about when to buy and sell it.

4: Learn about Capital Gains and Capital Losses

WHEN IT COMES TO THE STOCK PRICE, IT'S IMPORTANT TO NOTE THAT A COMPANY'S STOCK PRICE DOES NOT REFLECT THE TRUE VALUE OF ITS BUSINESS.

The stock price reflects the sentiment (feelings & opinions) of the market. In the short term, that means that the stock price depends on how the company is perceived by investors in the market.

If they like the company and are more willing to buy its shares, the stock price will go up.

If they are not impressed by the company, the share price may go down, because fewer investors are willing to buy its shares.

Even though the investors in the market have their ideas of what companies are worth, that does not mean that they are correctly estimating the value of each company.

To know what is the true value of a business, a special analysis of each company should be done, which will not be covered in this workbook.

Some prudent investors take time to research companies and value them before investing. Sometimes they find that a company is undervalued by the market and its price is low, when in fact it should be higher.

This represents a great opportunity to buy shares of this company when the stock price is low, and wait until the share price increases in value, so they can earn a profit.

CHAPTER 5:

Discover Dividends

DISCOVER DIVIDENDS

When it comes to investing there are two most common ways to earn money:

1 Buying an investment at a low price and selling for a higher price (we discussed this in the previous chapter)

2 When the business pays us dividends

WHAT ARE DIVIDENDS?

Dividends are payments that investors receive from a company whose shares they own. In short, dividends are distributions of company profits to the shareholders.

To illustrate this, let's use Mike's lemonade business as an example.

In the previous chapter, we talked about the company doing well after five years of going public.

During that year, the company earned $10,000 in revenue and had expenses of $6,000. What is the company's profit?

REVENUE: $10,000.00

EXPENSES: $6,000.00

PROFIT: $4,000.00

The company's profit is $4,000 ($10,000 - $6,000).

Now the company has two choices of what to do with this money.

OPTION 1	Use ALL of the profits to expand the business even further and open new lemonade stands to make even more money in the future.
OPTION 2	Share SOME of the profits with the shareholders as a way of thanking them for their investment in the company by giving them dividends.

Some public companies choose a combination of the two options. They will keep some money for expansion or future projects while also paying out dividends to the shareholders.

Some new public companies often reinvest all their profits in further expansion rather than paying them out as dividends to shareholders. They choose to do this to grow and thrive more quickly. Examples of such companies include Amazon, Facebook, Google, etc.

5: Discover Dividends

Let's practice making some calculations!

Let's pretend that the lemonade public company decided to pay half of its profits of $4,000 as dividends.

How much would be paid out per share of stock? Remember the lemonade company has 10,000 shares.

($4,000.00 / 2) / 10,000 =

How much would Ava receive in dividends considering that she owns 2,500 shares of stock?

2,500 shares x dividend paid per share of stock =

5: Discover Dividends

HOW OFTEN DO COMPANIES PAY DIVIDENDS?

The earlier example illustrates dividends being paid out for the whole year.

However, most public companies pay out dividends quarterly (every three months), and the amount can change based on how much money they made.

In one of the earlier chapters, it was mentioned that stock exchanges are regulated spaces that have a lot of rules.

One common rule is that public companies have to file their financial statements quarterly.

5: Discover Dividends

WHAT ARE FINANCIAL STATEMENTS?

Financial statements are documents that show how well a company's business is doing.

They show things like:

- » REVENUE
- » PROFITS
- » SOME OTHER METRICS
- » EXPENSES
- » LOSSES

Why are public companies required to file their financial statements every three months?

This is done to help investors evaluate the profitability and performance of the company more frequently. It helps investors with their decision making, such as whether they should stay invested in the company or sell their shares.

The financial statements also help companies assess how well their business has done.

The companies decide to issue dividends based on their financial statements and business performance.

If they decide to issue dividends, they make an announcement so that the existing shareholders and other potential investors are aware of their plans.

5: Discover Dividends

DIVIDEND INVESTORS

It is very common for retirees or people nearing retirement to invest in companies that pay dividends.

Retirees like to rely on dividend income to cover their living expenses (i.e. groceries, utilities, etc.) since they may not have a steady employment income anymore.

Investing in these companies, however, isn't just for retirees. Younger people can invest in these companies as well.

Some young people like to use dividends to fund their future lifestyles, such as paying for their car, cell phone, or other living expenses.

You can consider if this is something that you would want to do. You may even want to use dividends to fund your wants like new toys or books.

5: Discover Dividends

HOWEVER, JUST BECAUSE YOU RECEIVE DIVIDENDS DOES NOT MEAN YOU HAVE TO SPEND THEM.

You can also reinvest dividends by purchasing more shares of the same company. This entails putting your money back into investing and using it to make even more money.

BLUE-CHIP COMPANIES

There are a lot of companies that pay dividends. Some of them are called blue-chip companies.

These blue-chip companies are usually:

- ✓ Well-established
- ✓ Well-known
- ✓ Reliable
- ✓ Reputable for quality
- ✓ Pay dividends
- ✓ Profitable in good times and bad

Coca-Cola and Walmart are two examples of blue-chip companies.

Why are they called blue-chip companies?

These companies, like blue chips in poker, are highly valued, which is why they are known as blue-chip companies.

DIVIDEND ARISTOCRATS AND DIVIDEND KINGS

If you are interested in investing in dividend companies, you need to learn about dividend aristocrats and kings.

DIVIDEND ARISTOCRATS

The companies that make this list are known to meet the following criteria:

- ✓ Consistently pay dividends every three months
- ✓ They have increased dividends each year for at least **25 years**
- ✓ They are part of the S&P 500 index, which tracks the performance of the 500 largest companies in the US

Not all blue-chip companies meet the criteria to become dividend aristocrats.

5: Discover Dividends

Most dividend aristocrats are usually:

- ✅ Large and established companies
- ✅ Pay out dividends regardless of the state of the economy
- ✅ Have steady profits
- ✅ Not growing very quickly anymore
- ✅ Recession-proof (even if the economy is not doing well, these companies are fine)

DIVIDEND KINGS

These are companies that only meet one criterion:

- ✅ Pay out dividends consistently for at least 50 years.

Some of the dividend kings are also dividend aristocrats, as they are included in the S&P 500 index and have paid dividends for more than 25 years.

5: Discover Dividends

Let's do some research!

WHERE CAN YOU FIND A LIST OF DIVIDEND ARISTOCRATS AND KINGS?

Online search: S&P Dividend Aristocrats Index

Go through the websites listed in the results until you find one that you feel comfortable using for your research.

You may find familiar companies listed on these websites such as Coca-Cola, McDonald's, Colgate, etc.

5: Discover Dividends

As you can see, most of the companies listed are well-established and typically in the food and beverage or hygiene industries.

These companies are recession-proof and their products are used by people regardless of how the economy is doing.

> Based on your research above, which dividend aristocrats or kings would you be interested in investing?

> Are you surprised to see some companies on the lists of dividend aristocrats or kings? If so, which companies? Why are you surprised?

CHAPTER 6:

Understand Market Concepts

UNDERSTAND MARKET CONCEPTS

INVESTMENT VOCABULARY & TERMINOLOGY

It is important that you comprehend the concepts discussed in this chapter. You may hear others talk about them or hear them in the news. You want to make sure that you feel at ease and understand them.

THE BULL MARKET AND BEAR MARKET

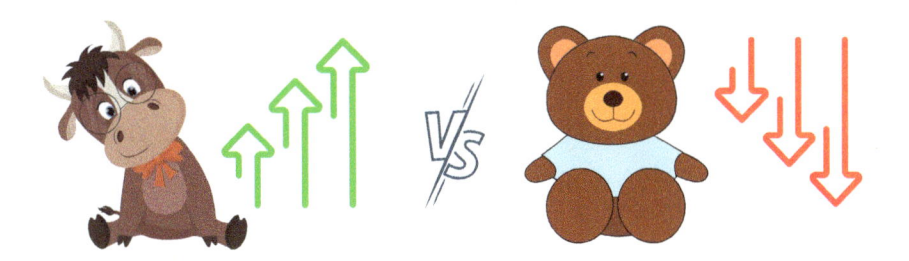

BULL MARKET	BEAR MARKET
• Market is doing well • Rising investment prices • Thriving economy • Decreasing unemployment	• Market is doing poorly • Stock prices fall • Economic slowdown • Increasing unemployment

A bull market refers to an economy that is doing well. Stock prices are generally high and keep rising. The economy is thriving.

A bear market is the opposite of a bull market. The economy starts to decline. Companies are not doing well, and their profits either decrease or they have losses.

Due to that, they let go of some of their employees, which causes increasing unemployment. Stock prices start to fall. Most people's investments are doing poorly, and many investors panic and sell their investments.

6: Understand Market Concepts

WHAT CAUSES A BULL OR BEAR MARKET?

A bull or bear market can be brought on by underlying economic factors such as the rate of inflation, unemployment and interest rates, and so on. It is also influenced by market sentiment, which refers to people's expectations of how well companies will perform going forward.

Just to give you an example:

2002 to 2007
There was a housing boom. The term 'boom' indicates that the economy was doing well.

2008 to 2009
The market crashed in the United States. The term "crash" refers to an economic downturn in which many people lost money and jobs.

2009 to 2020
The market was recovering, and the economy was picking up again.

Feb 2020 to Jul 2020
The market crashed once more as a result of a global pandemic, which restricted travel, trapped people at home, closed businesses, and so on, causing the market to perform poorly.

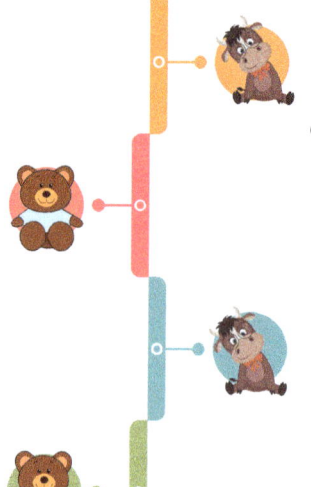

Aug 2020 to Dec 2022
As of August 2020 stock prices were rising, but then in 2022 there was a downward trend in the markets, and overall the stock prices were falling.

6: Understand Market Concepts

A BULL OR BEAR MARKET IS A CYCLICAL PHENOMENON.

This means that the market will always have ups and downs. It is also impossible to predict how long a bull or bear market will last. However, the economy has historically always grown.

MARKET CORRECTION

Before a bear market occurs, there needs to be something called a market correction.

Market correction happens when stock prices decrease more than 10% but less than 20%.

Market corrections can turn into bear markets when stock prices fall more than 20% from their highest price in one year.

Market corrections happen more frequently than bear markets.

6: Understand Market Concepts

MARKET CRASH

A *market crash* is different from a market correction.

It is a dramatic drop in stock prices in a very short period. For example, stock prices can drop 10% or more in one day.

This can be caused by a major catastrophic event and may trigger a bear market.

One example of a market crash was caused by the COVID-19 pandemic which started on March 9, 2020.

6: Understand Market Concepts

HAWKISH AND DOVISH POLICIES

HAWKISH POLICY

- Increase in interest rates
- To keep inflation under control

DOVISH POLICY

- Lower interest rates
- Stimulate economy
- Stimulate growth

Certain government organizations (policymakers) create rules which affect the economy. An example of this is when they increase interest rates to slow down inflation and prevent the economy from spiraling downwards, resulting in a prolonged bear market.

6: Understand Market Concepts

HAWKISH POLICY	DOVISH POLICY
The hawkish policy reduces people's desires to borrow money and invest as interest rates rise and the cost of borrowing money becomes higher.	The dovish policy is the opposite of hawkish. During this time, policymakers lower interest rates to stimulate the economy. When interest rates are lower, it makes it easier for people to borrow money.

When policymakers are dovish, they encourage economic growth.

Therefore more people are willing to borrow money and start businesses, buy homes, purchase vehicles, etc.

6: Understand Market Concepts

Let's have some fun learning!

Draw a line from each investment concept to the statement that applies.

Bull Market — Markets are doing poorly. Stock prices fall and unemployment is increasing.

Bear Market — Interest rates have been increased in order to keep inflation under control.

Hawkish — Interest rates are lowered in order to stimulate growth in the economy.

Dovish — The economy is thriving and investment prices are rising. Unemployment is decreasing.

6: Understand Market Concepts

INVESTMENT TERMS

Complete the word search puzzle below.
Have fun!

G	P	R	I	C	E	S	W	T	E	G	H	C	P
R	R	L	B	O	I	L	S	A	D	O	O	R	H
O	S	W	G	E	E	E	P	E	O	V	L	Y	O
W	T	L	N	T	R	M	C	H	V	E	M	C	T
T	O	N	A	E	C	O	T	S	I	R	A	I	H
H	C	R	T	I	N	H	S	I	S	N	R	L	R
L	K	N	E	O	W	E	L	K	H	M	K	O	I
L	I	W	M	O	B	H	G	W	W	E	E	P	V
A	H	Y	I	L	E	A	O	A	V	N	T	O	E
F	T	E	L	O	A	G	S	H	N	T	T	V	O
T	T	L	R	W	R	L	O	R	T	N	O	C	E
Y	A	O	O	E	E	T	A	L	U	M	I	T	S
L	O	O	H	R	S	I	A	H	I	G	H	E	R
P	B	U	L	L	N	O	I	T	A	L	F	N	I

BEAR
BULL
CONTROL
DOVISH
ECONOMY
FALL
GOVERNMENT
GROWTH
HAWKISH
HIGHER
INFLATION
INTEREST
LOWER
MARKET
POLICY
POOR
PRICES
RATE
STIMULATE
STOCK
THRIVE

6: Understand Market Concepts

CHAPTER 1:

Explore Different Investment Products

EXPLORE DIFFERENT INVESTMENT PRODUCTS

This chapter will briefly introduce you to some investment products.

Why is it important for you to know about this?

One day when you are ready to start investing, you may want to know what products are available for you to invest in.

Before this chapter, we only talked about investing in stocks of public companies, but you can invest in other investment products.

WHAT ARE INVESTMENT PRODUCTS?

An *investment product* is something that you put money into in hopes of earning profits.

The investment products that you choose to invest in will depend on the following factors:

☑ Your risk tolerance

☑ Your goals and time horizon (the length of time you expect to hold on to an investment before selling it)

Here is a brief explanation of each of those factors.

RISK TOLERANCE

When we invest there is always a risk that we can lose our money. Some investments are riskier than others. The risk is proportional to how much money can be gained or lost.

Some investments like stocks of public companies are riskier than keeping money in a savings account.

Make sure that you choose investments that are in line with your risk tolerance.

The general risk tolerance levels are:

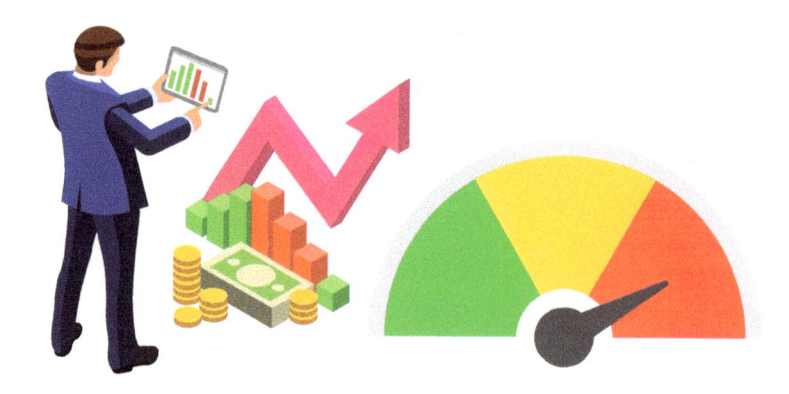

CONSERVATIVE

Conservative investors have a low tolerance for risk and investment losses.

MODERATE

Moderate investors are willing to take some risk of losses for higher returns.

AGGRESSIVE

Aggressive investors have higher risk tolerances and the ability to take an investment loss in exchange for higher returns in the long term.

7: Explore Different Investment Products

GOALS AND TIME HORIZON

Before you invest, you need to identify your goal.

- ✅ Why are you investing?
- ✅ What are you planning to achieve?
- ✅ Is this a long-term or a short-term goal?

For example, if you are investing to be able to purchase your first car, that may be a short-term goal if you are planning to purchase it in the next 2 - 3 years.

However, if you are investing to buy a home 10 years from now, that is a long-term goal, because 10 years is a long time.

We discussed bull and bear markets. As you know, markets are cyclical. They go up and down, but overall (historically) they have had an upward trend.

7: Explore Different Investment Products

95

SHORT-TERM INVESTING

When you are investing for the short term, your investment strategy should take into consideration that there is always a chance that the market may dip. It may not recover by the time you need to recoup the money from your investments to accomplish your goal. This may cause you to incur losses.

LONG-TERM INVESTING

When you invest for the long term, your investment strategy may be more aggressive, because your investments have time to recover from the downs of the market.

INVESTMENT PORTFOLIO

The investment products that you choose make up your investment portfolio.

An investment portfolio is like a basket that can hold various investment products, which you choose based on your goal and risk tolerance.

7: Explore Different Investment Products

DIVERSIFICATION

THE IMPORTANCE OF DIVERSIFYING YOUR INVESTMENTS

It is always good to make sure that your portfolio has a variety of investment products that behave differently. Therefore if one of them loses money, the others may earn money. This is reducing the risk of losing all your money. It is called DIVERSIFICATION.

THERE IS A SAYING "DO NOT PUT ALL YOUR EGGS IN ONE BASKET."

All that means is that you do not want to rely on only one investment product to help you achieve your goals in case that investment product ends up losing money.

There are various investment products out there. We will only briefly introduce them here.

The different types of investment products:

- ✔ Term deposits
- ✔ Bonds
- ✔ Mutual funds
- ✔ Stocks
- ✔ ETFs
- ✔ Index funds

7: Explore Different Investment Products

TERM DEPOSITS

A term deposit is set up by opening an account and depositing cash with your bank or a brokerage. Usually, your money is locked in for some time, and you receive minimal interest.

Term deposits are very similar to Guaranteed Investment Certificates (GIC) in Canada and Certificates of Deposit (CDs) in the US.

RISK LEVEL: SAFE/LOW-RISK

PROS	CONS
• Very little management by investors is needed • You can invest for different periods ranging from 30 days or longer	• Minimal growth potential • A penalty may apply if money is taken out earlier • Low interest rates

BONDS

Bonds work by lending money to the government or a company so that they can use it to fund their operations. They pay back interest to investors for allowing them to borrow money.

⚠️ **RISK LEVEL:** MODERATE-RISK

PROS	CONS
• Investors receive a set amount of interest (called coupons) once or twice a year • If an investor holds a bond until the maturity date (agreement end date), they will get all their money back in addition to the interest	• Access to money is somewhat limited as the money stays invested in a bond for a few years until the maturity date • If an investor sells the bond early, they may make or lose money depending on whether the interest rates are up or down

7: Explore Different Investment Products

STOCKS

The stock allows investors to become part owners of a company. The investors can profit from dividends or by selling the shares when the stock price is higher than what their purchase price was.

⚠️ **RISK LEVEL:** HIGH-RISK

PROS
- May have voting rights and participate in business decisions
- Can sell shares at any time
- Two ways to make money: share price increases and dividends

CONS
- Transaction fees apply when purchasing or selling stocks
- Potential to lose all or part of the invested money

MUTUAL FUNDS

Mutual funds combine money from many people and allow a professional manager to invest it in a mix of stocks and bonds.

⚠️ **RISK LEVEL:** LOW TO HIGH

PROS	CONS
• The portfolio is more diversified as it may contain stocks and bonds • A professional manager manages the mutual fund • Mutual fund units can be sold at any time	• Management fees can be very high • A large number of mutual fund managers never beat the average market returns

INDEX FUNDS & EXCHANGE-TRADED FUNDS

Index funds and Exchange-Traded Funds (ETFs) are two products. While they have a few differences, they are very similar, and that is why we will be discussing them together.

⚠️ **RISK LEVEL:** LOW TO MEDIUM

PROS	CONS
• Own a stake in some of the world's largest corporations at a much lower cost • Diversification by investing in hundreds of companies rather than just one • Lower fees • Great for long-term investing	• Choosing the wrong index fund or ETF to achieve goals

Index funds and ETFs have already premade compositions of investment products. They may hold hundreds or thousands of stocks that follow indexes.

If you don't know what indexes are, think of a TV news channel and the finance info running on the bottom of the screen (check out the photo).

An index, like Dow Jones (DOW), tracks the performance of the stocks of the largest 30 US companies like Facebook, Google, etc.

S&P 500 is another index that tracks the performance of the 500 largest US companies.

If you see the index in green and a positive amount next to it, it may mean that the companies which make up that index are doing well overall.

7: Explore Different Investment Products

103

If the index is in red with a negative amount next to it, it may mean that the companies which make up that index are not doing well overall.

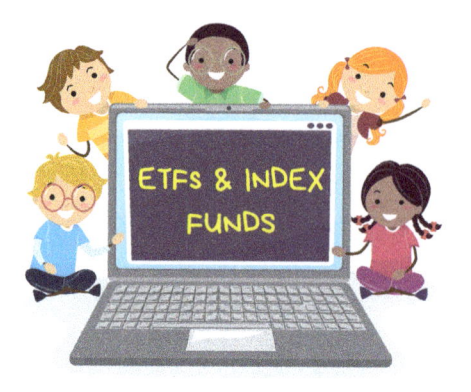

Now that you know what an index is, it's time to learn what index funds and EFTs are.

An index fund and an ETF are investment products that contain all companies which are part of an index.

For example, if you buy one share of an S&P 500 index fund or ETF, you will automatically invest in all 500 companies that the S&P 500 index follows.

You will have immediate diversification in your portfolio. With one share, you have invested in 500 stocks. If one company does not do well, the other 499 companies may make up for it.

SELECTING INVESTMENTS

Mike and Ava will show us how they pick their investments.

Mike is 14 years old and he wants to buy a used car 3 years from now. He wants to invest now so that he has enough money to buy the car when the time comes.

Mike in 3 years

GOAL: Buy a used car 3 years from now.

RISK TOLERANCE: Low to Medium

Mike's goal is short-term as it is 3 years from now. Since the market can be unpredictable in such a short period, Mike's risk tolerance is low to medium.

Therefore he chooses to invest half of his money in term deposits and half of his money in bonds.

7: Explore Different Investment Products

BONDS

TERM DEPOSITS

With this kind of portfolio, his investments are fairly safe. They may not earn him high interest, but even if the market does not do well over the next 3 years, the chances of Mike losing money are low.

Is that the best decision for Mike?

There is no way to tell until the 3 years are over because we cannot tell the future.

Mike has to make the most educated decision based on his risk tolerance and goals.

7: Explore Different Investment Products

Ava is 13 years old and wants to save money for graduate school after she obtains her university diploma. Her goal is approximately 10 years away.

GOAL: Save enough money for grad school 10 years from now.

RISK TOLERANCE: Low to Medium

Ava in 10 years

10 years is a long period, so Ava can afford to be more aggressive than Mike with her investments. Ava decides to invest in index funds.

INITIAL INVESTMENT

INDEX FUNDS

7: Explore Different Investment Products

Even if the market dips now or in the near future, there is plenty of time for the market and Ava's investments to recover.

> However, it is important to note that as Ava gets closer to her goal deadline, she will need to shift the composition of her portfolio to more conservative investments.

For example, a couple of years before she gets into a grad school, Ava should start selling some index funds and replace them with more bonds or term deposits. She will do this to avoid potentially losing money if the market experiences a downturn.

INDEX FUNDS → **BONDS AND TERM DEPOSITS**

Let's figure out what type of investor you are and what your investment portfolio would look like.

Online search: Free investment risk assessment tool

> Free investment risk assessment tool

From the listed results, pick one with the most reputable website, and complete it.

After completing the free risk assessment, circle your risk tolerance level:

CONSERVATIVE   MODERATE   AGGRESSIVE   OTHER

If you circled other, please write down what you got:

....

7: Explore Different Investment Products

What is your goal?

Is it short-term or long-term?

What investment products would you like to invest in and keep as part of your portfolio?

1. ....

2. ....

3. ....

4. ....

5. ....

7: Explore Different Investment Products

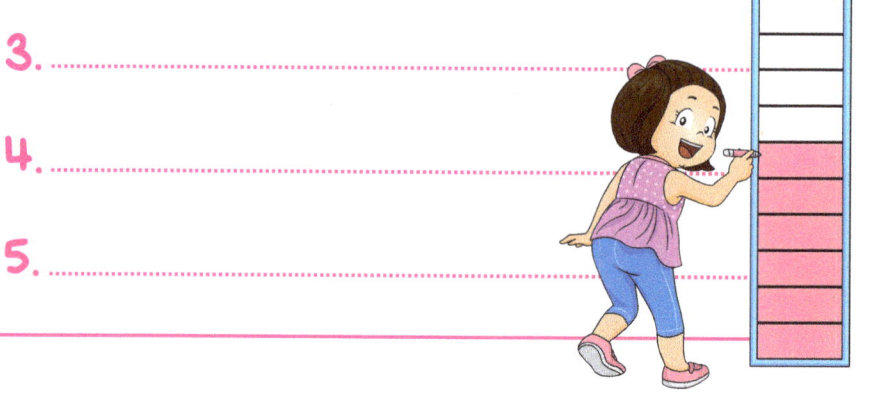

Answer Key

WHY SHOULD I INVEST?
Answer Key

CHAPTER 1 PAGE 6

Let's go back to pretending that you have $1,000. You decide not to purchase the computer. Instead, you want to save the money in a savings account.

Let's see how much interest you'll earn by keeping $1,000.00 in the savings account for the whole year if a bank gives you 2% interest.

> Please use the calculator or ask an adult for help with this calculation if this was not covered by your math curriculum yet.

Savings x Interest Rate = Interest Earned

$1,000.00 x 2% = $ __20__

How much money will you have in your savings account by the end of the year?

Savings + Interest Earned = Total Amount You'll Have by the End of the Year

$1,000.00 + $ __20__ = $ __1,020.00__

Answer Key

CHAPTER 1 PAGE 9

Let's go back to pretending that you have $1,000. You originally decided to save the money in a savings account for the year and buy the computer later.

Let's figure out what happened to the cost of the computer due to inflation over the year. For this example, we will use the inflation rate of 6.3%.

> Please use the calculator or ask an adult for help with this calculation if this was not covered by your math curriculum yet.

Computer Cost x Inflation Rate = Increase in Cost Over the Year

$1,000.00 x 6.3% = $ __63.00__

What is the total cost of the computer by the end of the year?

Original Cost + Increase in Cost Over Year = Computer Cost at the End of the Year

$1,000.00 + $ __63.00__ = $ __1,063.00__

Answer Key

CHAPTER 1 PAGE 14-15

Calculate how much money your investment of $1,000 will earn if you invest it at a 10% interest rate.

$1,000.00 x 10% = $100.00

You will earn $100.00 by investing $1,000.00 at a 10% interest rate.

Inflation is the rising cost of goods and services over some time.

Interest is the money you get back for letting someone use your money.

WHEN SHOULD I START INVESTING?
Answer Key

CHAPTER 2 PAGE 24

How long will it take for you to double your money if you keep $1,000.00 in a savings account at a 3% interest rate per year?

If you need help with this calculation, use the calculator or ask an adult.

72 / Interest Rate = Years

72 / 3 = __24__ years

CHAPTER 2 PAGE 25

For example, let's say that you want to double your money in 8 years. How much should your annual (yearly) interest rate on an investment be?

To calculate that, you need to divide 72 by the number of years you want your money to double.

If you need help with this calculation, use the calculator or ask an adult.

72 / Number of Years You Want Your Money to Double = Interest Rate

72 / __8__ years = __9__ %

Answer Key

CHAPTER 2 PAGE 27

What is the name of the concept that allows your money to earn money on already earned money?

(Please circle the correct answer)

a. Playing games

b. Compound interest

c. Magic tricks

The Rule of 72

is a quick way to calculate how long it will take to double our money if it is invested at a particular interest rate.

MEET THE KEY PLAYERS
Answer Key

CHAPTER 3 PAGE 34

Calculate the profit or loss of Ava's cupcake business. In December, just before the holidays, Ava purchased supplies to make cupcakes and spent $200. With those supplies, she baked the most delicious cupcakes, which she sold for $700.

Did Ava have a profit or loss for the month of December? If so, how much?

$700.00 - $200.00 = $500.00

Ava's cupcake business earned a $500.00 profit in the month of December.

If Ava repeated the same process from January to April, and each month she earned $700 in revenue but spent $1,000 in total on cupcake supplies, how much did she earn from December to April?

$700.00 x 5 months = $3,500.00 ← (Total Revenue for the months of December – April)
(Revenue each month)   (December – April)

$3,500.00 - $1,000.00 = $2,500.00 ← (Total Profit for the months of December – April)
(December – April Revenue)   (December – April Expenses)

Answer Key

When should I start investing?
Answer Key

CHAPTER 4 PAGE 60-61

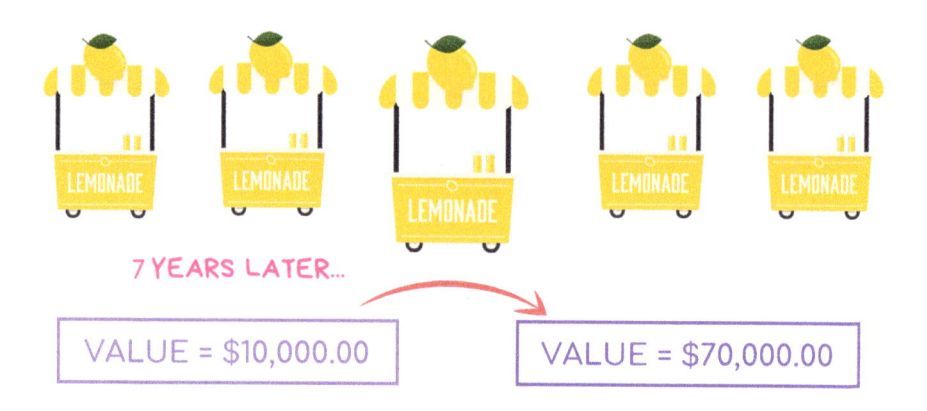

7 YEARS LATER...

VALUE = $10,000.00

VALUE = $70,000.00

Let's pretend that it is 7 years after the lemonade business went public. The business is still profitable and highly regarded by the market and other investors. They think that it is worth $70,000.

If there are still only 10,000 shares of the lemonade business, how much is each share of stock worth now?

$70,000.00 / 10,000 shares = $7.00

7 years after the lemonade business went public, each share of stock is now worth $7.00.

Answer Key

Help Ava calculate her capital gain if she sold her 2,500 shares at the new price of shares. Remember, she originally bought each share at $1/share.

2,500 shares x $7.00 = $17,500.00
(Ava's number of shares) (New price per share)

$17,500.00 - $2,500.00 = $15,000.00
(Ava's initial investment) (Ava's capital gain)

Ava earns $17,500.00 and has a capital gain of $15,000.00 by selling her stocks 7 years after initially buying each share of stock at $1 per share.

If Ava is doing this calculation for fun but does not sell her shares, is her capital gain realized or unrealized?

Ava's gain is unrealized because it has not happened yet.

Answer Key

When should I start investing?
Answer Key

CHAPTER 4 PAGE 63-64

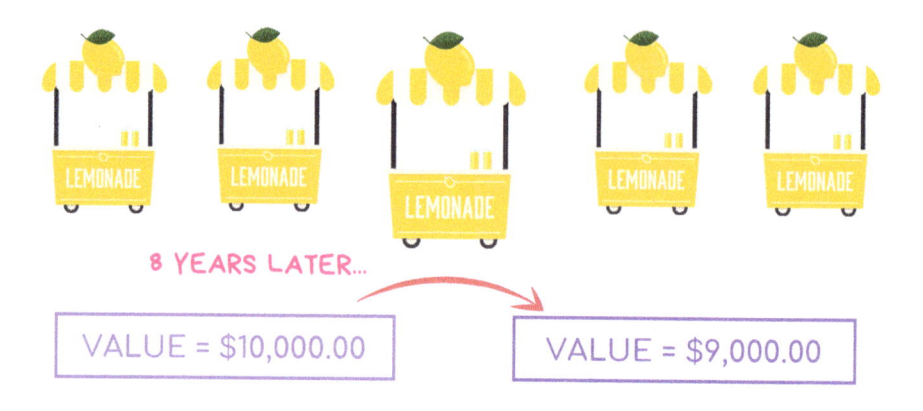

8 YEARS LATER...

VALUE = $10,000.00

VALUE = $9,000.00

Let's pretend that it is 8 years after the lemonade business went public. The business is not doing well anymore. It has suffered significant losses. The market and other investors think that it is worth $9,000.

If there are still only 10,000 shares of the lemonade business, how much is each share of stock worth now?

$9,000.00 / 10,000 shares = $0.90

8 years after the lemonade business went public, each share of stock is now worth $0.90.

Ava thinks that the lemonade business will continue to do poorly in the future. She wants to cut her losses and decides to sell her shares before they are worth even less. Calculate Ava's capital loss when she sells all 2,500 shares at the new market price of shares. Remember, she originally bought each share at $1/share.

2,500 shares x $0.90 = $2,250.00
(Ava's number of shares)   (New price per shares)

$2,250.00 - $2,500.00 = -$250.00
          (Ava's initial investment)   (Ava's capital loss)

Ava earns $2,250.00 but suffers a capital loss of $250.00 from selling her stocks 8 years after initially buying the shares at $1 per share.

Is this loss realized or unrealized?

Ava's capital loss is realized as she decided to sell her shares at $0.90.

Answer Key

Discover Dividends
Answer Key

CHAPTER 5 PAGE 72

Let's pretend that the lemonade public company decided to pay half of its profits of $4,000 as dividends.

How much would be paid out per share of stock? Remember the lemonade company has 10,000 shares.

$4,000.00 / 2 = $2,000.00 ← (The total amount given out as dividends)

$2,000.00 / 10,000 shares = $0.20

The lemonade public company is giving out $0.20 per share of stock as dividends.

How much would Ava receive in dividends considering that she owns 2,500 shares of stock?

2,500.00 shares x $0.20 = $500.00

Ava will receive $500.00 in dividends because she owns 2,500 shares of the lemonade public company.

Understand Market Concepts
Answer Key

CHAPTER 6 PAGE 89-90

Draw a line from each investment concept to the statement that applies.

Bull Market → The economy is thriving and investment prices are rising. Unemployment is decreasing.

Bear Market → Markets are doing poorly. Stock prices fall and there is a higher rate of unemployment.

Hawkish → Interest rates have been increased in order to keep inflation under control.

Dovish → Interest rates are lowered in order to stimulate growth in the economy.

Answer Key

INVESTMENT TERMS

Complete the word search puzzle below. Have fun!

G	P	R	I	C	E	S	W	T	E	G	H	C	P
R	R	L	B	O	I	L	S	A	D	O	O	R	H
O	S	W	G	E	E	E	P	E	O	V	L	Y	O
W	T	L	N	T	R	M	C	H	V	E	M	C	T
T	O	N	A	E	C	O	T	S	I	R	A	I	H
H	C	R	T	I	N	H	S	I	S	N	R	L	R
L	K	N	E	O	W	E	L	K	H	M	K	O	I
L	I	W	M	O	B	H	G	W	W	E	E	P	V
A	H	Y	I	L	E	A	O	A	V	N	T	O	E
F	T	E	L	O	A	G	S	H	N	T	T	V	O
T	T	L	R	W	R	L	O	R	T	N	O	C	E
Y	A	O	O	E	E	T	A	L	U	M	I	T	S
L	O	O	H	R	S	I	A	H	I	G	H	E	R
P	B	U	L	L	N	O	I	T	A	L	F	N	I

BEAR
BULL
CONTROL
DOVISH
ECONOMY
FALL
GOVERNMENT
GROWTH
HAWKISH
HIGHER
INFLATION
INTEREST
LOWER
MARKET
POLICY
POOR
PRICES
RATE
STIMULATE
STOCK
THRIVE

124 Answer Key

Notes

Chapter 1, pages 6, 9, and 10

The calculations are based on December 2022 inflation rate and average savings account interest rates in Canada. These numbers are comparable to the US inflation rate and average savings account interest rates for the same time period. Please refer to the bibliography for detailed resources.

Chapter 2, page 21

The example with Silvia and Mary assumes that each of them invested in an index fund that follows S&P 500. The 10% rate of return was assumed as the annualized return with dividends reinvested. Please refer to the bibliography for resources.
Purposefully, no inflation rate was used in this calculation to illustrate the large difference between the end amounts.

Chapters 1 to 7

All the calculations of profit exclude taxes. The concept of taxes was excluded for easier comprehension by the reader.

Bibliography

Maverick, J. B. (2023, February 15). S&P 500 average return. Investopedia. Retrieved March 6, 2023, from https://www.investopedia.com/ask/answers/042415/what-average-annual-return-sp-500.asp

Barnea, A. (2022, December 31). Banks charge more than 6% on loans, but give less than 2% on savings accounts. Are we being gouged? thestar.com. Retrieved March 6, 2023, from https://www.thestar.com/business/opinion/2022/12/31/cash-held-in-registered-savings-accounts-at-the-big-5-banks-continues-to-earn-surprisingly-low-interest-as-borrowing-rates-keep-rising.html

Government of Canada, Statistics Canada (2023, January 17). Consumer price index, December 2022. The Daily. Retrieved March 8, 2023, from https://www150.statcan.gc.ca/n1/daily-quotidien/230117/dq230117a-eng.htm?HPA=1

Iacurci, G. (2023, January 12). Here's the inflation breakdown for December 2022 - in one chart. CNBC. Retrieved March 8, 2023, from https://www.cnbc.com/2023/01/12/heres-the-inflation-breakdown-for-december-2022-in-one-chart.html

Dow Jones & Company (2022, December 14). The Fed's latest rate hike means 'fantastic' savings rates. Are you still earning less than 1%? The Wall Street Journal. Retrieved March 8, 2023, from https://www.wsj.com/buyside/personal-finance/fed-rate-hike-december-2022-high-yield-savings-cd-rates-01670868279

Additional Resources

Investment Roadmap

Are you ready to elevate your investment strategy?
Take the first step towards achieving your financial goals by downloading the <u>FREE Investment Roadmap</u>. This comprehensive guide provides a clear and concise step-by-step plan to help you navigate the next steps in your investment journey.
Visit www.InvestmentWorkbook.com to get started today and embark on a path toward financial success with confidence and ease.

Wealthy Kids Investment Club

Ready to become a savvy investor and grow your wealth? Join the Wealthy Kids Investment Club!
This membership program offers beginner-friendly investment strategies and resources to help you succeed.

Sign up and receive a FREE online course and workbooks on How To Teach Your Child To Become a Millionaire.

Visit www.WealthyKids.club to register and start investing with confidence.

Social Media

Join Maya's community on social media to receive daily tips on how to educate children to become financially independent adults. Follow her today to stay informed and empowered!

Instagram: @teach.kids.money
YouTube: Teach Kids Money TV
Facebook: Dinarii Financial Education Academy
Twitter: @Educ8Money2Kids
TikTok: @teachkidsmoney

Acknowledgments

Without the help of many people, this book would not exist. It would also not look as beautiful and kid-friendly if it was not for the hard work of Cyra K. Thank you for all your effort.
M.K. Williams, thank you for your guidance and support throughout the publishing process, without which this project would have been considerably more challenging.

Brad Darling, your meticulous fact-checking and insightful feedback on simplifying investment jargon and other complex topics were incredibly helpful.
Maria Revoredo, thank you for double-checking the math in the book and ensuring its accuracy. Your expertise was invaluable.

Nicky Savic, your advice on how to make this book more interesting for children was precious. Thank you for all your detailed feedback. I wish I had you as my English teacher when I was younger.
Shaylene Finch, I know that you are a busy mom, so thank you for finding time in your packed schedule to review the book and provide valuable feedback.
Iva Slezic, thank you for taking the time to go over the book with your kids and offer suggestions on how it can be improved.
Sujata Sikka, I appreciate your support over the years in various aspects of my business, especially for finding the time to go through the book with your children and provide helpful suggestions.

Jessica Smith, thank you for taking the time to review the book. Your feedback was very helpful.

Suzanne Tomory, big thanks to your family for joining my testing crew, and helping me make the book better.

Verica Savic-Jovcic, I appreciate that you and your girls are always willing to help me out and participate as testers for my content creation.

Delia Emelyanov, thank you for your assistance with the introduction of this book. I hope to meet you one day in person.

Last but not least, my amazing family. You have always been supportive of my wild dreams and never doubted me, but encouraged me in my pursuits. To my kids for allowing me to experiment on them with different teaching methods and for being the test subjects for this book and for all my other content creations.

To my mom, dad, and brother for believing in me and being proud of me, which has always made me push and work harder. I feel fortunate to have your unwavering support.

To my amazing husband, my best friend, who is my sounding board. Thank you for your patience and for always being willing to listen to my business adventures. Thank you for proofreading all my content, for the advice, and for always jumping in when I need an extra pair of hands to help with work.

ARE YOU READY TO TAKE THE NEXT STEP IN YOUR INVESTMENT JOURNEY?

If so, download the FREE Investment Roadmap.

This comprehensive guide will show you an easy step-by-step plan that you need to consider before investing.

Visit www.InvestmentWorkbook.com to get your free guide now.